GERMANNESS ON TRIAL

The German Evangelical Synod of North America
and the Espionage Act of 1917

A Paper Presented to the American Society of Church History
at Grand Rapids, Michigan, on April 9, 2011.
Revised With New Information November 2024

DR. CHARLES A. MAXFIELD

Germanness on Trial

The German Evangelical Synod of North America
and the Espionage Act of 1917

by Dr. Charles A. Maxfield

Copyright © 2025

Library of Congress Control Number:
International Standard Book Number: 978-1-60126-989-8

SANTOS BOOKS

TABLE OF CONTENTS

PREFACE

On November 18, 2001, a Sikh temple in Oswego County, New York, was burned to the ground. Three teenagers, inflamed by anti-Arab rhetoric following nine-eleven, and lubricated by beer, decided to act. They were unaware that Sikhs are not Muslims. In February 2002, a Syracuse area physician was arrested for operating an Islamic charity that provided food and medical supplies to people in Iraq. The climate of anti-Iraqi feeling in and outside the courtroom contributed to the conviction of this administrator of a charity.

I am a historian. The events of 2002-3 felt strangely similar to events of 1917-8. In both cases the government had decided to begin a war that could not be justified by just war theory. In both cases, the government mounted a propaganda campaign to convince the American people that this was a good idea. This entailed creating a climate of fear and hatred of the enemy. Some of the venom of this hatred would be directed at Americans who identified with the enemy ethnic or religious group. Can't we learn anything from history!

One small Protestant German-American denomination was overwhelmed by this tsunami of propaganda, vigilantism and legal action in 1917-8—the German Evangelical Synod of North America. This is their story.

THE ARRESTS

On July 31, 1917, a warrant was issued for the arrest of John Reichardt, German-speaking pastor of Zion German Evangelical Church of Lowden, Iowa, for violation of the new Espionage Act.[1]

On August 30, 1917, a Deputy Marshal boarded a train in Steubenville, Ohio, and arrested Dr. Paul Krusius, German-speaking pastor of Saint John's Evangelical Church, Monroe County, Ohio. Krusius was bound for Chicago to accept a teaching position at his denomination's college at Elmhurst. As Krusius was not an American citizen, he was never charged or tried, simply placed in an internment camp for the duration of the war.[2]

On November 6, 1917, federal agents arrested German-speaking pastor John Fontana, of Peace Evangelical Church, New Salem, North Dakota, for violation of the Espionage Act of 1917.[3]

On December 1, 1917, authorities arrested Wilhelm Schumann, German-speaking pastor of First German Evangelical Church of Pomeroy, Iowa, for violation of the Espionage Act.[4]

The German Evangelical Synod of North America was under attack. What had these pastors done that caused their neighbors to see them as a threat to the peace and security of the United States? How does a religious denomination cope, when its ethnicity causes it to be identified with the nation's enemy?

The transcripts of the two trials that were actually held, reveal the nature of the pastors' crimes, and the character of American "justice" when pressed by war hysteria. Behind the scenes, the various factions of this ethnic denomination struggled over the best way to survive the war.

THE WAR

For two and a half years the United States followed a path of professed neutrality while the great powers of Europe did their best to destroy each other in the Great War. During this time of neutrality, Americans could cheer for whichever side they wished. On April 6, 1917, war was declared, and this all changed. The United States had taken a side, and to support the other side was disloyal.

German Americans, many of whom read German-language newspapers and some of whom had relatives in the German army, saw events in Europe differently from America's pro-war English-language newspapers. Nevertheless, German Americans were overwhelmingly loyal to their adopted land in its war against their fatherland.

The decision to go to war was neither obvious nor unanimous. There was no "Pearl Harbor," no "nine-eleven;" no incident that shocked and united the country. Before the declaration of war, the people debated. Many opposed war from religious or socialist perspectives. The vote for war in Congress (82-6 in the Senate; 373-54 in the House of Representatives) revealed significant pockets of reluctance.

In a century of total war, when all citizens would be called upon to make sacrifices for their country, governments had to mobilize public opinion. A population that believed in a war brought social pressure on its young people to register for the draft and willingly put themselves in harm's way. People needed to be convinced that these deaths had a purpose. The federal government created the Committee of Public Information[5] on April 13, with the object of propagandizing the country for the war. Speakers crisscrossed the country, persistently repeating unsubstantiated atrocity stories of what the barbaric "Hun" (German) had done. It should not be surprising that a nation stirred up to fever pitch to kill Germans might look unsympathetically at their German-speaking neighbors.

German spies were everywhere—so people believed. America mobilized to hunt them down. On March 22, 1917, the Bureau of Investigation (BI) of the Department of Justice authorized the organization of the American Protective League (APL).[6] This voluntary secret society of a quarter of a million spy-catchers, not finding many spies, turned to exposing "slackers"—persons not sufficiently enthusiastic for the war. German Americans, socialists, reformers, trade unionists and conscientious objectors caught their attention. APL operatives did provide information to the government, which sometimes led to legal action. Much more often they carried out direct actions: tar and feathering, forcing someone to kiss the flag, painting someone's door yellow (the color of cowardice), and other acts of humiliation.

Congress passed the Espionage Act on June 15, 1917. Sections 1 and 2 of the Act described activities of information gathering that spies might do. Section 3 stated:

> Whoever, when the United States is at war, shall willfully make or convey false reports or false statements with intent to interfere with the operation or success of the military or naval forces of the United States or to promote the success of its enemies, and whoever, when the United States is at war, shall willfully cause or attempt to cause insubordination, disloyalty, mutiny, or refusal of duty, in the military or naval forces of the United States, or shall willfully obstruct the recruiting or enlistment service of the United States, to the injury of the service or of the United States, shall be punished by a fine of not more than $10,000 or imprisonment for not more than twenty years, or both.[7]

As judges and juries took up cases, "false reports or false statements" came to include any statement critical of the war effort, and any such criticism was assumed to "willfully obstruct the recruiting or enlistment service of the United States."

The German Evangelical Synod of North America defined itself as a "unionist" church. Although of predominantly Lutheran background, it sought to include both Lutheran and Reformed traditions. Created by missionaries of the Basel and other Lutheran-Reformed missionary societies, it identified theologically with the Evangelical Church of the Union of Prussia and other German states—the Kaiser's church. Before the war, the Evangelical Synod often called the Prussian Union Church their "mother church," and received most of their members through immigration from that church. Once the United States entered the war, the Evangelical Synod emphasized that there was no formal connection—no line of accountability—to the Kaiser's church.

The Synod was German-speaking. Most congregations worshiped in German. District and Synod meetings were conducted in German, reports were published in German, most articles in their *Theological Magazine* were written in German. Evangelical Synod pastor Hugo Kamphausen, in a 1924 book describing the Synod to its brethren in Germany, wrote of these days:

> On Good Friday, 1917, Congress adopted a resolution declaring that a state of war existed between the United States and Germany. It was the darkest Good Friday in German-American history! During the early years of the war German Americans had frequently and strongly taken a stand, particularly also in the public press, in support of Germany. Now that America had identified itself with the Allied cause, this would not be forgotten. Americans became obsessed by a stupid and unfounded but none-the-less virulent fear of spies. And every German-American was looked upon as a potential spy and enemy of America. If he had been for Germany earlier he no doubt still was, so it was said. His sympathies, it is true, were still with Germany. But it was not true that he was an enemy of his

adopted country. On the contrary the German-American knew what his duty was and did it. He gave his sons to fight in the American armed forces. He placed his money on his country's altar. That he did not do all this as gladly as the Anglo-American was of course true. How could it have been otherwise?

There was directed against him, however, the senseless fury of a whipped-up highly incensed public opinion.... The Germans lived in an atmosphere of hatred under the vigilant eyes of suspicious neighbors. Things became worse after the infamous Espionage Act was adopted. Now written and oral expressions were subjected to censorship and severe penalties provided for such as were deemed indicative of disloyalty. Hardly a word could be said or printed that was not subject to misinterpretation by evil-spirited individuals always with the threat of dire consequences for the person concerned.[8]

THE INVESTIGATION

The Bureau of Investigation (BI) of the Justice Department received a letter on April 10, 1917, claiming that Pastor John Reichardt, the postmaster, and another German American at Lowden, Iowa, were "acting and talking in an un-American manner."[9] On May 14 the Division Superintendent urged the United States Marshal at Dubuque, Iowa, to "investigate at the first opportunity."[10] An agent visited the town on May 29, and interviewed several persons, but did not locate the pastor. He reported the town "evenly divided on the war question," but saw no need for further action.[11]

On April 19, 1917, agent H. G. Garber went to New Salem, North Dakota, to investigate complaints that Rev. John Fontana, on the Sunday after the United States entered the war, prayed for the success of German arms. The agent interviewed Fontana and reported:

> The Rev. Fontana told agent that up to the time that he actually knew that war had been declared by the United States that he prayed for the success of the German arms, but that he did not do so afterwards. That he still hopes for the German arms to a certain degree, but not against the United States.[12]

The "Americans" around New Salem had heard that Fontana prayed for Germany on that Sunday, but the agent could not find a witness who attended that church service who could confirm that rumor.[13]

In the summer of 1917 Special Agent John B. Wilson of Wheeling, West Virginia, investigated complaints against Dr. Paul Krusius, pastor of Saint John's Evangelical Church, Switzerland Township, near Powhatan Point, Ohio. He reported that Krusius,

In a sermon stated that he hoped every transport carrying American troops to France would be sunk and every soldier drowned, and further that he hoped no American soldiers who went to Europe would live to return. An investigation proved that he was very pro-German and that the community was very wrought up against him. He was apparently trying to stir up the German people in the community against the United States. Krusius had stated that he had been in England after the outbreak of the war and posed as a Russian in order to leave there. It was also rumored that he had been in South America just prior to coming to the United States....[14]

As Krusius was not an American citizen, he did not at that time have the right to hear the charges against him, confront his accusers, or have his day in court. As an enemy alien he would simply be interned for the duration of the war.

The BI received a letter from attorney F. F. Faville of Pomeroy, Iowa, on October 26, 1917, complaining that Rev. William Schumann of Pomeroy was "quite pro-German and has been making manifest his leanings in the neighborhood and among his parishioners."[15] The BI office in Omaha received a more detailed complaint, dated November 13, 1917, from Edwin Wattonville, Pomeroy postmaster:

Rev. Wm. Schumann, pastor of the German Evang. Lutheran Church, Pomeroy, Iowa, is reported to have asked his congregation from the pulpit to not buy Liberty Bonds. He has refused to contribute to the Red Cross and as a reason for doing so he said there was dishonesty and graft in the society....

Schumann stated, that when he took out his citizenship papers he did not swear to defend the constitution of the U.S.A. to the extent of fighting Germany, and that under no circumstances would he fight for this country against Germany....

Prior to the declaration of war he was very active working in the interest of Germany by circulating petitions to the
Government, urging them to stop shipments of ammunitions
to England and France. He circulated many of these petitions,
also had cards printed, which he circulated and solicited sign-
ers to, which were sent to our Senators and Representatives by
him, urging them to keep out of war. This was done at the time
the twelve Senators were blocking action in Senate.

He is the moving spirit of all German propaganda carried
on in this community, he associates with Germans only, will
have nothing to do with the American people and brands the
American Press as Liars.

He has stated that he has five brothers in the German
Army and that they are all officers.... We consider this man a
menace to the community and he should not be at large.[16]

Schumann's efforts to petition Congress were clearly within
his rights. However, on the basis of the other complaints the Department of Justice sent Special Agent Werner Hanni from their Omaha
office to investigate. A Swiss-born American citizen fluent in German, Hanni was responsible for investigation of pro-Germanism.
He spent a week in Pomeroy interviewing people, and at the end of
the week attended the worship service, on November 11. Another
Special Agent, John McAuley, came to arrest the pastor on December
1. McAuley interviewed Schumann at his home, and in the smoking
car of the train from Pomeroy to Fort Dodge, during which time
Schumann expressed his views freely.

Reinhold Niebuhr, a young Evangelical pastor in Detroit and
a strong supporter of the war, came briefly under suspicion in November 1917. He was reported to be "strongly pro-German in his
sympathies," and his mail was monitored.[17] The intelligence officer at
Camp MacArthur was notified to "be on the look-out" for him. On

December 9 a "loyal American" was sent to a service for soldiers and congregants that Niebuhr addressed at Waco, Texas, and reported, "he said nothing that could be construed as disloyal."[18]

Herman Hahn, a 30-year-old Evangelical Synod pastor, outspoken Socialist and anti-war activist, served Saint John's Evangelical Church of Millersburg, Ohio, 1913 to 1916. According to an interview given many years later, "public indignation drove him from his church."[19] He then went to Toledo and edited a Socialist paper, *The People's Press*. BI agents attempted unsuccessfully to confiscate the April 20, 1918 issue, which criticized the Liberty Bond drive.[20] According to the later interview, "Government agents shut down his newspaper. Vigilantes finally chased him from the city in which he lived."[21] Hahn appears to have disappeared at this time. On May 8 authorities searched and confiscated two boxes of Hahn's personal effects from the American Express Company. These included several anti-war speeches.[22] Somehow Hahn evaded authorities and was never indicted.

THE CHARGES

Reichardt, Fontana and Schumann were indicted under the Espionage Act. With what crimes were these pastors charged? John Reichardt of Lowden, Iowa, was indicted for certain things that he said on July 15, 1917, in a sermon at his church:

> 'that this country (meaning the United States) is in war with Germany without any cause and by reason of the American officials being dishonest and untruthful, and because said American officials believe what is printed about the war in American newspapers, all of which are lies, that the truth about the war is printed in the German newspapers; that the charges made by the officials of America and the American newspapers of atrocities committed by the soldiers of said Imperial German Government in Belgium were all lies; that America had no business in this war and that Germany had a right to do the things it was doing; and it was his (meaning himself, the said John Reichert's) duty to tell the people of his congregation all about such things,' and other statements of the same import and meaning...

These were considered "false statements with intent to promote to success of...the Imperial German Government," and "obstruct the recruiting and enlistment services of the United States."[23]

This indictment referred to comments Reichardt was alleged to have made in a sermon on a Sunday following a Fourth of July celebration which distressed his German American congregation. The main speaker at the community's celebration spoke in graphic terms of brutal atrocities German soldiers were alleged to have committed.[24] Reichardt spoke to reassure his hearers that not everything that was said was true.

John Fontana was charged by a grand jury for things he said at New Salem, North Dakota, "on or about" December 19, 1917, although he had been arrested on November 6, and received a preliminary hearing on November 27. He was charged under the Espionage Act for making false statements and obstructing enlistment in the military, by:

> falsely stating that President Wilson was a man who after securing his election on the slogan 'kept us out of war' turns squarely around and by the use of his high office of President whipped the members of Congress into line by threats of exposure of this one and that one and in this way secured the authority to enter into war with Germany; that he felt proud of the noble fight the Germans were making in the war; that the sinking of the *Lusitania* was justified and that there was no reason whatever for the United States taking up arms against Germany; that he frequently and as a minister of the German Evangelical Church prayed for the success of the armies of Germany over the armies of the United States...; that he did not want to subscribe for Liberty Loan Bonds because it would tend to encourage the administration; that the President was using the same methods of threats to force every bank in the United States to subscribe to Liberty Loan Bonds; that the purchase of Liberty Loan Bonds would give the country more money to fight Germany and thus prolong the war; that he desired the success of the enemies of the United States.[25]

The indictment of Wilhelm Schumann cited the Espionage Act and named some enlistment-age men in attendance when Schumann gave a sermon on November 11, 1917. The indictment presented an English translation of statements Schumann allegedly made in that sermon:

That the war in which America is engaged is for the capital-
ists only and the Liberty Bond is a great humbug, by buying
Liberty Bonds you buy yourself deeper into slavery; America
went into this war to help England; that America had no right
to go into this war against Germany and that Germany was
right; that he was asked to take up a collection for the Red
Cross but we could raise our own money and send it to our
own Germans and help them out; that it was a money war and
men were making money out of it; that he did not believe in
the YMCA at all, that it is gotten up by the Methodists and I
want my people to stay away from it and stay by the Lutheran
church; that our boys should not go over and shed their blood
to help England.[76]

Three pastors of the Evangelical Synod, Reichardt, Fontana
and Schumann, were charged with saying in sermons, and in private
conversations, words that could harm the United States. In normal
times, we in the United States consider it our right to criticize our
government. As we read these charges with the comfort of distance in
time, nothing they are alleged to have said sounds criminal. But in a
time of war, a populace that has been manipulated by a government
propaganda campaign, and that is looking for the enemy within, will
see non-conforming opinions as criminal. Judges and juries are not
immune from the mood of the country, and will be influenced by it.
But did these pastors actually say the things they were alleged to have
said? Or was the language they spoke and loved sufficient to make
them criminals? Or at least make it possible for people to believe any
accusations made against them, and to not believe any defense they
might make?

Two of these four pastors had their day in court. These cases
reveal to what extent the pastors had integrity, and to what extent the
courts could resist the pressures of popular opinion.

EXTRA-GOVERNMENTAL ACTIVITY

Two of these pastors experienced the wrath of the enemies of all-things-German in their communities, where people did not wait for judges and verdicts before they took action. On December 3, 1917, two days after his arrest, a crowd of 150 persons marched to Pastor Schumann's residence in Pomeroy, Iowa, raised the American flag there, required him to salute it, and ordered him to not take it down.[27] Asked by community leaders to leave town, he replied that he would leave when he was ready. Threatened with violence, he replied that he was prepared for the worst.[28] The *Pomeroy Herald* concluded: "It is up to Schumann as to whether he leaves Pomeroy, in a quiet or peaceful way, or whether he takes his chances of being forcibly ejected. From all indications, he will not be given a great deal of time to decide either."[29]

On New Year's Eve the German Evangelical Church of Pomeroy burned to the ground. In the judgment of the congregation, as noted in their minutes, "criminal hands and a fanatic mob had committed a work of darkness."[30] On January 8, fearing trouble, Schumann called the county sheriff for help. The paper reported, "The minister was confronted in a store by a committee of loyalists who pulled a watch and said that he had one minute to announce that he would leave town that day."[31] Schumann agreed and a deputy sheriff soon arrived to provide him escape. For some time Schumann was in hiding. Descendants of church members still repeat stories of his hiding on the farms of various parishioners.[32]

Church leaders brought charges against the arsonists, but a grand jury refused to indict them, the judge ruling "extenuating circumstances" were involved.[33]

Schumann continued to serve his congregation, meeting in homes and in groves, while the construction of a new church building moved forward. Following the laying of the cornerstone on September 29, 1918, trouble resumed. One night in late October a brick came through a window of Schumann's home, striking the head of the bed in which he slept. On November 1, two of the local "patriots" were looking over the construction site; Schumann asked them to leave. The following day they were back again. Edwin Wattonville, postmaster, and William Weyganat, restaurant keeper, arrived on the scene; two persons believed by the congregation to be the arsonists and the principal instigators of trouble for Schumann. The Pastor told them to leave. They refused. Schumann threw a brick at them and they retreated to the street. A few more bricks passed in both directions. Wattonville attempted to re-enter the building, at which time Schumann and he "mixed it up." Construction workers pulled them apart. Wattonville sued Schumann for assault.[34]

In Lowden, Pastor Reichardt continued to serve Zion while his case passed through postponements. On Armistice Day, November 11, 1918, a mob gathered in Lowden to take out their anger on the Germans. Pastor Reichardt was forced to march through town with the flag, stand on a coffin (representing the demise of the Kaiser) and kiss the flag. Then they ordered him out of town. He spent the night in the security of a jail cell at the county seat.[35]

PERSONALITIES IN COURT

The two cases against Evangelical Synod pastors that went to court were contested by competent and experienced attorneys. The federal district attorneys took the lead in prosecution, while the Synod secured skilled attorneys to defend the pastors.

The Prosecutors

FRANK ALOYSIUS O'CONNOR (1875-1954) led the prosecution in the Schumann trial. Aged 42 years, O'Connor had been a United States attorney for the Northern District of Iowa since 1914. He received his LL.B. degree from the University of Iowa, served as county attorney for Chickasaw County (1903-1907), as a Democratic member of the Iowa State Legislature (1909-1912), and was currently serving on the Governor's National Defense Board, responsible for defending Iowa in the war. He had moved from Chickasaw County to Dubuque in 1918, where he would become active in Democratic Party politics, and in the affairs of the Roman Catholic diocese.[36]

MELVIN A. HILDRETH (1859-1944), age 58, had been U.S. attorney for North Dakota since 1914. Hildreth was admitted to the bar at Watertown, New York, in 1883, and in 1888 moved to Fargo, Dakota Territory. He was a judge advocate in the Philippines following the Spanish American War, and served as city attorney of Fargo 1892-1894 and 1902-1904.

Hildreth was one of the founders of the Democratic Party in North Dakota in 1889, and at the 1908 Democratic National Convention gave a seconding speech for William Jennings Bryan. He was Inspector General of the North Dakota National Guard 1905-1908. Hildreth belonged to the Episcopal Church.[37]

Hildreth indicted more persons under the Espionage Act, in proportion to the population of his district, than any other U.S. attorney. Only four states, all with much larger populations than North Dakota (Texas, California, New York, and Illinois) had more cases.[38] North Dakota politics at the time was dominated by the Non-Partisan League (NPL), a populist agrarian movement that included many known Socialists. The North Dakota branch of the American Protective League had targeted the NPL, and many of the cases initiated by Hildreth prosecuted NPL spokespersons.[39]

For the Defense

COMFORT HARVEY VAN LAW (1869-1947), age 48, led the defense of Schumann. Born in Iowa, son of a Quaker, Van Law received his B.A. degree from Iowa State University in 1896, taught political science and economics there and in two years received his M.A. Admitted to the bar in 1897, since 1898 he had practiced law at Marshalltown, Iowa. He was city attorney for Marshalltown 1901-1905, and represented that area as a Republican in the State Senate 1909-1912. He was admitted to practice before the Supreme Court in 1904.[40]

JOHN KNAUF (1868-1952), age 50, defended Fontana. Knauf was born in Michigan to Prussian-born parents. He received his law degree from the University of Michigan Law School in 1892. The following year he was admitted to the bar at Jamestown, North Dakota, and became active in Republican politics. He served as judge of Stutsman County beginning in 1894.[41]

In 1906 Knauf was appointed to fill a vacancy on the state Supreme Court. At that time Alexander McKenzie's Republican political machine, supported by the Northern Pacific (NP) Railroad, dominated North Dakota politics. In his legal practice Knauf often represented clients with grievances against the NP. In the 1906 campaign for judge, following his appointment, several Fargo lawyers issued statements that Knauf was a "boozer and a libertine" (in reality he did not drink). Without the support of his own party, Knauf lost the election,[42] having served on the state Supreme Court only four and a half months. Knauf returned to private practice and gradually regained his reputation. Throughout the Fontana trial the court respectfully called him "Judge Knauf."

The Judges

HENRY THOMAS REED (1846-1924), age 71, presided at the Schumann trial. A practicing lawyer since 1870 at Crescona, Iowa, and a Republican state representative in 1876, Reed was appointed to the Bench by Theodore Roosevelt in 1904.[43]

CHARLES FREMONT AMIDON (1856-1937), age 61, grew up in western New York state, son of a Methodist circuit rider. Upon graduation from Hamilton College in 1882, he went West to organize a high school in the new settlement of Fargo, Dakota Territory. Amidon studied law, was accepted to the bar in 1887, and had become a Democrat. In 1896 he was appointed Judge of the North Dakota District.

Zacharias Chafee, in writing about the trend to interpret the Espionage Act loosely, to the detriment of free speech, said, "A few judges, notably Amidon of North Dakota, swam against the tide."[44] Geoffrey Stone, in *Perilous Times*, lifted up only three district judges who defended free speech during World War I; Amidon was one of them.[45]

On June 13, 1918, Amidon rejected the indictment of E. H. Shutte, who was alleged to have said, "this is a rich man's war and it is all damn graft and swindle . . . if you do not believe it, just look at the cost of wheat." In rejecting the indictment Amidon ruled:

A valid indictment must embrace three facts: 1. The language must have been willfully uttered.... 2. The language itself must have been of a character to cause some of the results denounced by the law.... 3. The language must have been uttered on an occasion such that a reasonable man could say that it might produce one or more of the results mentioned in the act....[46]

John H. Wishek, a prominent pioneer, politician and banker, was indicted for distributing a pamphlet, *German Achievements in America*, and allegedly speaking critically of Liberty Bonds. Amidon charged the jury to ask if he did anything with the intent to hurt the war effort. A hung jury on July 22 led to the charges being dropped.[47]

Job W. Brinton, an NPL organizer, was indicted for a speech in which he denounced war profiteering. District Attorney Hildreth accused Brinton of fomenting class warfare. Amidon declared,

I have never known any great reform being carried through where the people whose established condition would be disturbed by the carrying out of the reform did not say that the people who were trying to bring about the reform were stirring up class against class. That is an argument that I know to be at least 3,500 years old....If it could prevail we never would get any change in an existing condition.[48]

Amidon directed a not guilty verdict. Amidon presided over these three cases within two months of the commencement of the Fontana trial. Amidon was under considerable personal stress, as his daughter later wrote,

Sometimes friends and neighbors of a lifetime crossed the street to avoid speaking to him. One Sunday morning when he took his seat in church, the two people in the pew got up and moved across the aisle. He received threatening letters. More than once, a person he called on the telephone refused to speak with him.... [49]

The Defendants

WILHELM SCHUMANN, age 37, was born at Usseln, Germany, on November 19, 1880. He came to the United States in 1898 and became a naturalized citizen in 1904. After attending the Evangelical Synod Seminary at Saint Louis, he served churches in Hamilton, Illinois, Ledyard, Iowa, Jackson County, Minnesota, Aurelia, Iowa, and since 1912 Pomeroy, Iowa. All of his parishes belonged to the Evangelical Synod, and they all worshiped in German.[50]

JOHN FONTANA, age 46, was born at Altshausen, Germany, on January 20, 1872, to an Italian father and German mother. He came to America in 1888, and studied theology at a Lutheran seminary at Afton, Minnesota. He was ordained in 1893 and served congregations of the Evangelical Synod in Ohio, Webster, South Dakota, Norwich, Minnesota, and Albany, Minnesota. He had been serving Peace Church, New Salem, North Dakota, for nine years. He became a citizen in 1898. Fontana had an American-born wife and five children.[51]

The trial of Pastor Wilhelm Schumann was held at Fort Dodge, Iowa, on June 21, 1918. Defense Attorney Van Law moved that the charges be dropped. The charge was dropped that accused Schumann of attempting to cause "insubordination, disloyalty and refusal of duty to the military forces of the United States." But the second count of the indictment remained that he did "obstruct the recruiting and enlistment services of the United States."

The prosecution called four witnesses: Department of Justice Special Agent Werner Hanni, who had attended the worship service of November 11, 1917, two church members who also attended that service, and Special Agent John McAuley, who arrested Schumann on December 1. The first three testified that Schumann made the statements alleged in the indictment, although the two church members could not swear that he said all those things on that day.

The defense was limited by the court to presenting only four other witnesses in addition to the defendant, who was the first witness. The four other witnesses, all church members who were in attendance on November 11, 1917, all denied that Schumann made the statements that he was alleged to have made.

When Pastor Schumann testified about his November 11th sermon, he explained that it was given on the 400th anniversary of Martin Luther's birth,[52] on the text, "Ye shall know the truth and the truth shall make you free." He presented Luther's concept of Christian freedom. He spoke of the courage of Luther in the face of the all-powerful Papacy, and how Luther was called all sorts of names. He used an illustration:

> I said it is something like in our days, in our days England
> and Russia had the power, were world powers, and they had

divided the world among themselves—and the German com-
merce, and Germany wanted a place in the sun also, and then
Germany was called the disturber of the peace....[53]

A collection was taken that Sunday for the Synod's seminary and
Schumann urged support saying, "You have considered it your patriotic duty to buy Liberty Bonds, now also buy these liberty bonds,
or this kind of liberty bond to spread the real freedom, the truth to
obtain the real freedom...." [54]

The Defense argued that these statements had been taken out
of context to imply something very different from their intent.

When Prosecutor O'Connor asked one of the prosecution
witnesses about Schumann's attitude toward the use of the German
language, and Van Law objected, O'Connor explained:

> Well I think my idea is that it all bears upon the state of mind
> at this time at a time when this country was concerned in a
> war with Germany, and statements made contemporaneously
> with this that this was a rich man's war or a capitalistic war or
> an unjust war, that we should preserve the German language
> and talk it in the church and talk it in the home would all
> be calculated to the particular thing complained about in the
> indictment, that is to obstruct or would tend to obstruct the
> enlistment and recruiting service of the Country and which is
> all a part and parcel of the testimony that bears upon the intent
> and the state of mind of the man.[55]

Judge Reed replied, "Well you have been permitted to share all that with
the exception of the use of language." The language issue was declared
out-of-bounds, but otherwise, the transcript abounded with testimony
relative to the "state of mind" or "mental attitude" of Schumann.

McAuley's testimony all pertained to "state of mind" as it oc-
curred after the date mentioned in the indictment. McAuley's mem-

ory of his conversation with Pastor Schumann in the smoking car of the train was as follows:

> Mr. Schumann says 'We Germans do not believe that the United States has any right to get into the war, that the United States was in the war simply to help England,' and in arguing with him I advanced the idea that perhaps the atrocities in Belgium might offer an excuse for the United States to be in the war, and he said that he didn't believe that there were ever any atrocities committed in Belgium; and the matter of sinking ships came up, and he said that he didn't think that was an excuse for the United States to be in the war, that the first American ships were sunk by English mines, and in regard to the sinking of the *Lusitania* he said that that was absolutely right it should be sunk too, it was a munition ship and a floating fortress; he said that the United States was in the war simply to aid England and that because the Americans had loaned England money, or that England had sold bonds in America, and America was getting in the war to protect that money. He told me in the course of this conversation that he had five brothers in the German army, and that if he was in Germany he would be in the army, probably in the Prussian Guard on account of his physique.[56]

Pastor Schumann remembered the conversation differently,

> I asked him if he really believed that there were German spies in those little places like Pomeroy, and well he said—I told him we had no way of connection with Germany, and how we could be of assistance to Germany, and then he said the German submarines they sink all the English ships and the Germans will come over and then we suppose the Germans in this country will be friendly to them; and then I told him if he never heard anything about German faithfulness, when a German gives his word he respects it, and we told him we Germans had sworn allegiance

to this country and we would keep our word, and even if my own brothers would come and would invade our rights I would fight them, that is what I told Mr. McAuley, and then he said, he asked me what do you think about the *Lusitania* affair, and I told him what Mr. Stone had said about that, the Senator Stone, and then he asked me what do you think about the Belgian atrocities and I said Mr. Shepard, American reporter, said that he never could get a first hand atrocity story.... [57]

Prosecutor O'Connor pushed Pastor Schumann as to whether the views of the authorities he cited were his views, to determine his "state of mind." Finally O'Connor asked, "What was your view at that time of the cause of the war?"[58] Van Law objected and was overruled. Schumann at first refused to answer, until directed to do so by his attorney. He said,

> Well I am not in favor of war, and when the war started in 1914 I worried a great deal for I am not in favor of war at all, and then my sympathies went with Germany, that is the country of my birth, and I considered the cause of Germany right, and then when we entered the war it was a very hard feeling for me, and we consider Germany our mother and we consider America our bride, and it isn't a normal state of affairs when mother and bride are in quarrel, and if I—well I—I just the same considered it my duty to support this country, and even if I had to support it with a bleeding heart, for we as Christians we know we have to be—have to be obedient to the Government.[59]

In O'Connor's mind, this talk of a "bleeding heart" indicated a divided loyalty, which contradicted the oath taken at naturalization—that a person renounces all former loyalties and will be loyal to the United States alone. Schumann explained, "There are ties made by God, and my mother is still living over there in Germany, and I would do my duty as a citizen and would fight against the land of my birth, but I would do it with a bleeding heart."[60] Schumann explained that he did not believe the atrocity stories because "My brothers are in the war and I know they wouldn't commit any crimes like that."[61] Through the interrogation, Schumann affirmed that he believed he should work for peace, but at the same time had a duty as a citizen to support this country's war effort. He indicated he had as an individual, and as leader of his church, supported various fund drives for the Red Cross and YMCA, but always through denominational channels, and he supported the sale of Liberty Bonds. O'Connor's interrogation continued:

Q. But you still entertain the opinion that you are against war, you still entertain that opinion?

A. I think war isn't a normal state of affairs, and if we have a right to work for war in time of peace we always have a right in time of war to work for peace.

Q. And that is the principal upon which you have proceeded in Pomeroy since the 6th of April among your people, that is in time of war you have a right to talk peace?

A. I don't remember that I talked about peace, but that is what I—what I want, I want peace.

Q. Now what was your viewpoint with respect to this country sending its boys or its troops across the ocean and to Europe to engage in this war, what was your viewpoint upon that question?

A. Well I wasn't in favor of it.

Q. Well you haven't changed your opinion about it have you?

A. What?

Q. You haven't at any time changed your opinion about it?

A. Well now, now it is my duty as a citizen to support the law—

Q. No, you haven't answered my question. (Question read to the witness follows: "You haven't at any time changed your opinion about it?")

A. I am against war, that is all, and I don't like to see the—to see the war and it would be—I would be—I would rather see it if the boys had stayed here, but now if they have to go, if the Government orders them, I support the Government.[62]

Judge Reed in his instructions to the jury explained that a person is innocent until proven guilty and the burden of proof is on the government. The jury first had to determine if Schumann actually did say what he was alleged to have said, and second, if he said it with intent to obstruct military recruitment. Reed defined *obstruct* as:

> any conduct on the part of any one by any word or act which retards, hinders, impedes or makes more difficult the efforts of the Government in recruiting, enlisting or otherwise bringing men of proper age into the service of its armies, navies and other military forces... [63]

The jury found Pastor Wilhelm Schumann guilty. Comfort Van Law had given Schumann a good defense. He petitioned at the commencement of the trial that the indictment was faulty, when prosecution rested he petitioned that a verdict of not guilty be directed because prosecution had not proven its case, and he appealed the verdict. In the course of the trial he made 56 objections, which he followed with exceptions.

U.S. V. FONTANA

The trial of Pastor John Fontana commenced on July 30, 1918, at Bismarck, North Dakota. Defense Attorney John Knauf issued a demurrer, a petition that the indictment be rejected as faulty, because (1) it did not state that Fontana had done anything illegal, (2) it did not give enough information for the defendant to know what he was accused of, in order to prepare a defense, (3) it did not state whom he influenced to be disloyal, (4) it did not give the time and place he was alleged to do certain things, and (5) there was no law against criticizing Liberty Bonds.[64] Judge Charles Amidon rejected this appeal. Knauf then petitioned that the prosecution be required to indicate on which of the several charges in the indictment it would depend for conviction. Motion denied, and the trial began.

It was a lively trial of three days' duration. Attorney Knauf made 124 objections for the defense, some of which were sustained. At one point Judge Amidon warned prosecutor Melvin Hildreth to be less violent in his speech.

Hildreth in his opening remarks stated,

> This human character that you have before you is a German character. He has prayed in the German language, and preached and sung in the German language. His soul is a German soul, while his body is here in America. He has enjoyed constitutional liberty under a free government since this war commenced; but his whole labor has been in one direction, that of aiding and abetting the land of his birth—Germany.[65]

The first witness for the prosecution, J. Henry Kling, cashier at the First National Bank of New Salem, reported on an interview he had with Fontana on October 24, 1917. Kling visited Fontana at his home in support of a Liberty Bond drive. His testimony, interrupted by frequent objections, follows:

> I went up there, and asked—I had a list along with me, and asked if he would put his name down on the list, showing him that I had already been to the schoolhouse and had all the teachers heading the list, and I wanted to have the preachers follow the teachers....
>
> I spoke to him in that way, 'I would like to have you head the list because of your influence in this town;' and I told him that...I would have no trouble after that to sell any of the members of his congregation. And he said no, he didn't want to do anything to use his influence to help out the present administration in this war because of the fact that President Wilson was elected on the slogan, 'He kept us out of war,' and then afterwards he used his power as president, his influence as president, to put us into war, by threatening exposure of certain congressmen. And I asked him how he could expose any congressmen. He said he had influence on all of them; all he had to do was to tell this man or that man, members of congress, that he would expose them to the light, and in that way he forced them to take a stand with the administration on this proposition—forced the country to war, and that the majority of the people were against war. For that reason he felt he did not want to buy any Liberty Bonds or use his influence that way because it would just tend to prolong this war. That is the substance of the conversation, and I could not—then as I sat there I noticed the picture of the Kaiser on the wall. That made me think of another question to ask him, and I asked him if he was acquainted with the Kaiser, and he said he knew him....
>
> He said that he knew the Kaiser to be a man of peace. That he had kept peace in Germany for over forty years, and at the present time there was no need for any war; that the Kaiser had offered peace on several different occasions, and all they had to do was to accept those terms, and there would be no war....

Well, we mentioned the *Lusitania*, and Reverend Fontana said that the sinking of the *Lusitania* was a humane act on the part of Germany, because of the fact that there were munitions on board, and by the sinking of the *Lusitania* it saved a lot of lives in Germany, and we would do the same thing....

One of the things I remember especially was the fact that he said, 'I am very proud of the fight the German people are making, can't help but be proud of it.' [66]

When Pastor Fontana testified, he presented a very different memory of the interview:

He came to the door and asked me if I had some time. I said I was just busy. 'Well,' he says, 'it will not take only a few minutes.' Well, I says he should come in, and he said he was there to get me on the list as Liberty Bond subscriber. I told him that I could not buy any Liberty Bonds. He says, 'Why not?' I said, 'Because I haven't got the money.' 'Oh,' he says, 'you got all kinds of money.' I says, 'I have not; I am in debt.' He says, 'Well, you got a rich congregation.' I said, 'The congregation's money isn't my money.' He says, 'We will make it easy for you. We will loan you the money.' Well, I asked him if he would loan it at the same rate of interest as the Liberty Bond was. He said, no, but they would make a very low rate of interest; would only charge me six percent; until after New Years, and after that ten percent. 'Well,' I says, 'I have a family; I can't afford to do that, and pay that high rate of interest, and buy Liberty Bonds. I cannot see my way through; I don't know how to pay it afterwards.' 'Well,' he says, 'but you ought to buy a Liberty Bond. If everybody would says that he could not afford to buy, we would not sell any.' I says, 'Other people have more money than I.' Then he says, 'Why don't you want to buy any Liberty Bonds? Don't you think it is a good investment?' I says, 'I do. I wish I had a lot of money; I would invest it in Liberty Bonds.

31

The United States is the best security there is in the world at the present time; and besides, if I had the money, I would not buy any Liberty Bonds from you.' 'Why not?' he says. 'Well,' I said, 'because I would buy the bonds where I do business, the bank I do business with.' Then he inquired about the Draft Law, what I thought of the Draft Law. I said, 'I think it is a very good law, and we ought to have had that law a couple of years before we entered the war. The people would be prepared then.' ... [67]

Upon further questioning Fontana denied all of the accusations of Kling, except that they did have some discussion of Wilson's election slogan and getting the country into war, and Fontana's belief that most Americans did not want the war. The only other witness to this conversation was Mrs. Fontana, who was present for part of the conversation, and whose testimony supported her husband's.

The trial meandered across a wide range of subjects and accusations. Amidon ruled that statements of the defendant about matters not in the indictment were "admissible as going to the defendant's *intent*."[68] Judge Amidon did create some boundaries. Fontana could only be convicted on things he said and did after the passage of the Espionage Act, June 15, 1917. Other earlier expressions or actions could show *intent*, but no expression of pro-German feeling before the Declaration of War, April 6, 1917, was relevant. On the other hand, anything Fontana did of a patriotic nature after the indictment of February 27, 1918, was inadmissible as potentially self-serving. When Knauf asked draft age young men on the witness stand if Fontana had influenced them against doing their duty, Hildreth objected and was sustained, because the Espionage Act made the *intent* of the defendant illegal, not the actual result.

A sermon illustration, which Fontana used on August 5, 1917, was lifted up by prosecution witnesses as evidence of his pro-German feeling. In a sermon on the subject of temptation, Fontana said,

"Germany has a weapon with which she held out against her numerous and powerful enemies until now; but God has given the Christian a weapon with which he can resist and overcome temptation at all times—the prayer."[69]

After considerable discussion of whether or not Fontana prayed for victory for Germany, he produced the Evangelical Synod's *Agenda,* or Prayer Book, and showed the court the prayers he used, prayers for the United States and for peace.

Nellie Dietz testified that Fontana did not support the Red Cross. Fontana explained he would not support the Red Cross at that time because he had read in *Issues and Events* a reprint from an article in the New York *American* of June 10, 1917, to the effect that the head of the American Red Cross, a Mr. Davidson, had said that the American Red Cross would not give aid to German and Austrian soldiers who fell behind Allied lines. He later read a retraction of that statement and joined. Judge Amidon then lectured him on the merits of the Red Cross.[70]

D. A. Podoll, a former Sunday School teacher, complained about a meeting Fontana had with the teachers asking them to use more German in the Sunday School. Fontana explained that he was responding to complaints from elders and parents, and acting in obedience to the church's constitution.[71]

There was considerable discussion about the relationship between the Evangelical Synod and the state church of Prussia. Fontana's finances were explored in depth. Hildreth questioned several witnesses about a meeting at the parsonage with Attorney Knauf in preparation for the trial.

Hildreth tried to prove that Fontana joined in a celebration of a victory of Germany over Italian forces in the Fall of 1917. All that could be proven was that three couples gathered for a social evening about that time.[72]

Reference to the pulpit Bible the church had received as a gift of the Kaiser was disallowed as no one could testify that it was used after the Declaration of War.[73] Likewise, no one other than Kling could recall seeing the Kaiser's picture on the wall at Fontana's home after the Declaration.

A United States flag, a "service flag" with a star for each member of the congregation in the service, and patriotic music in the worship service, did not appear until after Fontana was indicted.

Fontana explained that the second Sunday after war was declared he said to his congregation,

> Our country is at war with Germany now and we have to stand by this country. We have sworn that when we became citizens, and we have to stand by this country under all circumstances because this is now our Fatherland. We have no rights and no duties over there any more, and we have to stand by our country with all that we are and what we have to the last man if necessary.[74]

Fontana testified, "I have never been in favor of war... I am a man of peace."[75] Thirty-three young men from his congregation were in the Armed Services of the United States.

At the conclusion of the presentation of testimony, Knauf again petitioned that the charges be dropped, and was again turned down. Knauf, in his final argument to the jury reviewed the testimony against Fontana and concluded, "The burden of the government to prove the case has not been met. It is not met as to time, it is not met as to intent, it is not met as to sayings which could be held in violation of the statute."[76]

Hildreth, in his final speech to the jury proclaimed,

> In times of war the unbridled tongue is more dangerous than the army of the enemy, more stealthy than the submarine or aero-

plane. Does not all history point to this truth? The Government is engaged in a war that is testing the strength of its institutions as they have never been tested. Regardless of party, religion, or other environment, all men and women are contributing their money and labor, while across the seas the best blood of the land is being shed, to accomplish the one great purpose—the defeat of German autocracy. But here in the United States that same government has to fight a battle. Scattered everywhere throughout the land are the churches of Germans. Not that all are disloyal, but many were made disloyal. Not that the sons of many did not go to war, but that the sons of many might be made luke warm, weak and vacillating in the support of the government by the acts of such men as this man.[77]

Amidon had several times explained, "All these other things lying outside of the language that is the basis of this indictment are received for the purpose of showing the intent with which the defendant used that language and for no other purpose."[78] In his final charge to the jury Amidon reviewed the charges in the indictment and pointed out that the only solid testimony to most of the charges was from bank cashier Kling, from his personal interview with Fontana in Fontana's home.

After five hours of deliberation the jury returned the verdict: guilty.[79]

Court reconvened on Monday, August 5, for sentencing. Knauf again petitioned that the verdict be set aside because the indictment was faulty, to no avail. Amidon asked Fontana for a statement. He said,

I am not guilty. I never had an intention to say or do anything against the United States. I believe that what I have said has at least been misunderstood, and misconstrued. My sympathies

varied somewhat in favor of Germany before the United States
entered the war; but since the United States entered the war I
was first and last for the United States, and that means also for
their Allies. I am a citizen of the United States for twenty years.
My wife is born in this country. Her parents are born in this
country. My children are born in this country. I want to raise
them good citizens of the United States.[80]

Judge Amidon then interviewed Fontana asking several questions
about his background, then he lectured Fontana on his citizenship
vows, a lecture widely reproduced in papers across the country.[81]

By the oath which you then took you renounced and abjured
all allegiance to Germany, and to the Emperor of Germany,
and swore that you would bear true faith and allegiance to the
United States? What did that mean? That you would set about
earnestly growing an American soul, and put away your German soul. That is what your oath of allegiance meant. Have
you done that? I do not think you have. You have cherished
everything German, and stifled everything American. You have
preached German, prayed German, read German, sung German. Every thought of your mind and every emotion of your
heart through all these years has been German....

It [your Oath of Allegiance] does not mean simply that
you will not take up arms against the United States. It goes
deeper far than that. It means that you will live for the United
States, and that you will cherish and grow American souls in-
side of you. It means that you will take down from the wall of
your home the picture of the Kaiser and put up the picture of
Washington; .... It means that you will begin to sing American
songs; that you will begin earnestly to study American history;
that you will begin to open your lives through every avenue
to the influence of American life; it means that you will begin

first of all to learn English, the language of this country, so that there may be a door into your soul through which American life may enter....

When we get through with this war, and civil liberty is made safe once more upon this earth, there is going to be a day of judgment in these United States. Foreign-born citizens and the institutions which have cherished foreignness, are going to be brought to the judgment bar of this Republic....Every institution that has been engaged in this business of making foreignness perpetual in the United States will have to change and cease....That means a fundamental revision of these foreign churches. No freedom of the press will protect a perpetual foreign press in these United States. It won't protect any press or any church who, while it is trying to meet a temporary need, does not set itself earnestly about the business of making that temporary situation just as temporary as possible, and not making it, as has been true in the past, just as near perpetual as possible. Men who are not willing to do that will have to choose. If they prefer to cherish foreign ideals they will have to go to their own. If it is necessary we will cancel every certificate of citizenship in these United States....

And the object of the sentence which I pronounce upon you today is not alone to punish you for the disloyalty of which you have been guilty but to serve notice upon you; and the like of you, and all the group of people in this district who have been cherishing foreignness, that the end of that regime has come. It is a call to every one of you to set about earnestly the growing of an American soul in you.[82]

Under the Espionage Act, 1,956 persons were indicted, 877 convicted.[83] These are just two of those cases. Targets included participants in the Industrial Workers of the World (IWW), other trade unionists, the NPL, Socialists, religious and other conscientious opponents of war, members of the press, and leaders of the German-American community. Some had actually said or done things to discourage draft registration; others, like Schumann and Fontana, had done nothing. The Evangelical Synod was not the only church to suffer from anti-German feeling;[84] its association with "the Kaiser's Church," did make it a target.

From the safe distance of a century we can examine these trials with an objectivity that the participants could not have. We see a law being interpreted in such a way as to intrude upon basic civil rights, flimsy indictments, a lack of sufficient evidence, and guilty verdicts. We need to also see the torrent of social pressure created by government propaganda, vigilantism, and fear.

The actual legal prosecutions were only the tip of the iceberg of harassment. The APL claimed to have "brought to judgment three million cases of disloyalty."[85] The most common action was a humiliating flag-kissing ceremony before an unruly mob. A few incidents could strike fear into others. What will they do to me if I don't buy enough Liberty Bonds? If I read German newspapers? If I criticize the government?

Judge Charles Fremont Amidon is a puzzle for us to this latter day. How could he be so lenient with a Socialist rabble rouser denouncing Wall Street's War, then turn around with severity on a German pastor who couldn't afford to buy Liberty Bonds? The link between Progressivism and Nativism is not unique to Amidon. Teddy Roosevelt, the former progressive President, inveighed against hyphenated Americans at this time. Josiah Strong, in *Our Country* lifted up the perils of immigration while advocating social reform. Perhaps it would be more accurate to see Americanization as one plank of the Progressive platform for America.

Soul is a religious term. When Hildreth and Amidon speak of the need for an "American soul" this raises red flags in the minds of people of faith. Is America their god? Is this idolatry? Is patriotism seeking to supplant religious faith? Or are they simply saying that being American must sink more deeply and more thoroughly into their personal identities? Clearly patriotism does make demands of loyalty—especially in wartime—that people of faith would give only to God. Perhaps Amidon's language only makes transparent a form of idolatry that is usually more subtle.

THE INTERNMENT OF
PAUL KRUSIUS

Paul Krusius was born on January 15, 1879, at Ohligs, near Solingen, Germany. He had an interest in missionary work, and in 1899 went on an exploratory tour to the Libyan desert with Hermann K. W. Kumm. In 1900 Kumm launched the Sudan Pioneer Mission and Krusius acted as secretary until he began his university studies. Krusius studied at the University of Halle-Wittenberg from 1903 to 1909, receiving his Ph.D. in 1908 and passing his teachers' examinations in 1911 On May 1, 1911, he entered the service of the Sudan United Mission [SUM] as a missionary to northern Nigeria. The SUM had absorbed the Sudan Pioneer Mission and was headquartered in London, England. Krusius began a furlough in England by September 1913. He proposed to the SUM the establishment of a training institute in Nigeria for men and women from the mission stations to train them as evangelists and teachers. SUM approved the proposal and appointed Krusius to direct the institute at the conclusion of his furlough.[86]

Krusius was in the wrong place at the wrong time. The United Kingdom declared war on Germany on August 4, 1914. Anti-German riots soon followed across Britain; the government swept the country for German citizens, placing them in internment camps. As Krusius was unwelcome in Britain and the British colony of Nigeria, his plans were scrapped. I cannot trace the whereabouts of Paul Krusius for the next eleven months. He began pastoral work in the Evangelical Synod of North America on July 15, 1915. The Evangelical Synod was delighted to have someone in their midst with Krusius' academic credentials. In January 1917 he delivered a series of lectures at Eden Seminary related to missionary work with non-Christians. [87] Then the Synod appointed him to teach at Elmhurst College.

Interned at Fort Oglethorpe, Georgia, Paul Krusius searched his memory to try to recall anything he might have said or done that might be construed as disloyal. He pleaded for a fair hearing and for freedom. On November 5, 1917, he wrote to Attorney General Thomas W. Gregory:

> On August 30th, 1917, when about to take a train for Chicago, Ill., I was summarily arrested at Steubenville, O., by a Deputy Marshal as an alien-enemy, and taken to Columbus, O., and there interned in the common jail of Franklin County. The next day the U.S. Marshal, Mr. Devanney, told me that my arrest had been made by order of the President of the U.S., because my 'being at large in the Southern District of Ohio endangered the peace and safety of the U.S.' At the same time I was informed, that I would have no hearing nor any way of defending myself and that my confinement would probably last until the end of the war. After four weeks detention in the Franklin County Jail I was transferred to the War Prison Camp at Fort Oglethorpe, Ga., where I have been interned since.
>
> All this time I had been hoping that ere since I would be released, being confident, that a closer investigation of the circumstances that led to my arrest would show that I was not a person dangerous to the safety of the United States. I have tried to work among my constituency as a pastor with every discretion and carefully avoided everything political in my teaching and preaching. The only thing I am aware of that may, from the outside, be interpreted unfavorably, were a few remarks in an altogether private conversation with a young couple on the prospect of an early peace and that were made to alleviate their worry.
>
> Though I am not conscious of having infringed on the laws of this Country through what I said, I am very sorry, that I may have given offense to the authorities. My excuse is, that it was done without deliberation. Therefore I hope, that after

having been kept interned now for almost two months and a half, that my request to be released, or dismissed on parole will meet with a favorable consideration....[88]

His petition was denied. Krusius was never informed of the specific charges against him.

At the request of Army Chaplain J. H. Sutherland, Krusius assisted him at Fort Oglethorpe for the religious and general welfare of the camp.[89] On May 22, 1919, Krusius again wrote to the Attorney General from Fort Oglethorpe, asking if he could be released in the United States rather than being deported. He wrote, "The Department will be aware of the fact that I have never been connected with any German or Austrian interests nor have been engaged in any sort of Political activity or propaganda."[90] Again, the request was denied.

THE EVANGELICAL SYNOD

The Great War was the time of the Evangelical Synod's most severe testing. A few indictments for espionage, more numerous vigilante incidents, a climate of suspicion of all things German, and legal actions in some states against the use of the German language, all cast a shadow of fear over the Synod. Through its centralized but democratic structure the Synod defended itself against the external threat. At the same time, an internal conflict threatened the Synod. The war aggravated the existing tension between those who cherished their German heritage and those who wanted to be more American. The tension sometimes showed up between second-generation English speakers and first-generation German speakers, sometimes between the older congregations founded in earlier periods of immigration, and new congregations of recent immigrants. The tension existed within the hearts of individual German Americans who, like Wilhelm Schumann, loved both their mother, Germany, and their bride, America. But another tension arose within the more American element of the denomination—between the movement for Americanization and the Social Gospel with its prophetic and anti-war dimensions.

The German Evangelical Synod of North America was a small but growing denomination of over a quarter million communicant members in about a thousand congregations,[91] organized into nineteen districts, generally along state lines. The districts met annually; a General Conference of the whole Synod met every four years. Denominational headquarters were at Saint Louis, the historic center of the denomination. The Saint Louis group had absorbed smaller synods of similar background and belief centered at Chicago and Buffalo, and had spread with German settlement across the Great

Lakes and Ohio Valley regions, south to Texas, and westward into the prairie states. German immigrants and their children composed the congregations, growing through repeated waves of immigration. Like most immigrant churches, it was overwhelmingly working class.

From Saint Louis an elected President led the denomination in a pastoral manner, and a publishing house produced material in both German and English. The Synod's seminary at Saint Louis, unofficially called "Eden" Seminary, patterned after the schools of the German missionary societies, cultivated piety along with education. The Synod's school at Elmhurst, Illinois, commonly called a *proseminar,* prepared some young men for seminary, and others to teach in the Synod's parochial schools. The Synod also supported several hospitals and other institutions addressing human need, in most cases staffed by an order of Deaconesses, who were trained at Saint Louis.

The Synod President, John (Johann Friedrich) Baltzer (1857-1930), had grown up in the heart of the Synod and was well connected with its leaders. His father, Adolf Herman Frank Baltzer (1817-1880), educated at Berlin and Halle, came to America in 1845, pastored Evangelical congregations, taught at the seminary (1858-1866) and became President of the Synod (1866-1880), and editor of the Synod's parish paper, the *Friedensbote.* After Elmhurst and Eden, the younger Baltzer served parishes until elected President of Synod (1914-1929). American-born, although raised in a totally German-speaking environment, Baltzer worked to lead the Synod into the American mainstream, while being sensitive to the deep German cultural identity of the older generation and more recent immigrants.

Two trends of thought, usually progressing in tandem in Synod life, came into conflict as a result of the war: Americanization and the Social Gospel.

Americanization

The movement to Americanize the Synod had several concerns:

1. **Language.** To be truly American the Synod needed to worship in English, carry out its business in English, and conduct higher education in English. This major source of generational conflict produced anxiety for some older clergy who were unable to communicate clearly in English.

2. **Accreditation.** The *proseminar* at Elmhurst needed to become an accredited college, which would contribute to the status of the seminary. To accomplish this, several bright young men went to eastern colleges to get advanced degrees, in order to return to Elmhurst and Eden and reform their programs.

3. **Ecumenism.** The Synod needed to get out of its ghetto-mentality and cooperate with the English-speaking denominations. To build new ties of fellowship and cooperation, the Synod joined the Federal Council of Churches.

4. **Denominational name.** A movement to take "German" out of the name of the denomination had failed at the Synod's General Conference of 1917. The subject would soon be raised again.

5. **Church education.** Increasing numbers of the children of Synod members attended public schools. As a result, congregations relied less on their parochial schools and more on the Sunday School for Christian education. Americanizers placed steady pressure for English-language instruction and teaching materials.

6. **Prohibition.** At the Federal Council of Churches, the Evangelical Synod stood alone in its opposition to Prohibition. Americanizers wanted the Synod to get in step with other denominations in this movement.

7. **War effort.** Americanizers wanted the Synod to be "100%
American" in enthusiastic support for the war and its moral aims. This would bring the Synod into step with the rest
of American Protestantism and remove any cause for others to suspect the Synod of harboring disloyalty.

The General Conference of the Synod in August, 1917, created a War Welfare Commission to minister to Evangelical Synod
members in the military. The Commission named Reinhold Niebuhr
(1892-1971) its Executive Director. A graduate of Elmhurst, Eden,
and Yale Divinity School, Niebuhr, age 25, was pastor of Bethel
Evangelical Church in Detroit. With the help of his mother and his
sister he continued to serve Bethel while directing the Commission.[92]
The War Welfare Commission recruited Evangelical pastors living
near military training bases to visit the camps, provided religious
literature to the soldiers, and provided information to churches on
holding patriotic programs and memorial services.[93]

The Social View-Point

From its inception, the Evangelical Synod practiced the "Inner
Mission" as developed in Germany by Johann Hinrich Wichern, establishing hospitals, homes for the elderly and for orphans, and other
institutions for human need. Adolf Stoecker's work in Berlin and his
"Christian Socialism" also inspired some in the Evangelical Synod,
although they rejected his anti-Semitism.[94] In 1913 the Synod, with
the help of Eden students, founded Caroline Mission in a poor section of Saint Louis.

Julius Horstmann's 1934 article on "The Rise of the Social
View-Point in the Evangelical Synod," pointed to two authors who
inspired the movement, Josiah Strong and Walter Rauschenbusch. In
Our Country, Josiah Strong (1847-1916), according to Horstmann,

contended that the physical, earthly welfare of mankind was a fundamental principle of Jesus Christ, and that the neglect of this principle by a church intent only on the salvation of individual souls had alienated the masses of working people who were suffering from social wrongs.[95]

The work of Walter Rauschenbusch (1861-1918) was, according to Horstmann, "chiefly academic and theological,"[96] and did not have as great an influence on the church. Evangelical pastors did feel some kinship with Rauschenbusch, even if his father had become a Baptist. His father, Karl August Rauschenbusch (1816-1899) came to America from a German missionary society, became an agent of the American Tract Society and American Bible Society, and had visited many of the Evangelical Synod pastors of his era, selling his German-language tracts and Scriptures. In January, 1917, Walter Rauschenbusch had lectured at Eden Seminary.[97]

At General Conference in 1913, Julius Horstmann read a paper on "The Kingdom of God and Its Business in the Twentieth Century," the Conference created a Commission for Social Work, and the Conference adopted the "Social Ideals of the Churches," a statement of the Social Gospel adopted by the Federal Council of Churches in 1908.[98]

Julius Horstmann (1869-1954) led the Social Gospel movement in the Evangelical Synod. Born in America to German-born parents, he shared the Americanizing concerns of many of his generation. After graduation from Elmhurst and Eden, and serving churches in Texas and Indiana, he became in 1906 editor of the Synod's new English-language paper, *Messenger of Peace,* later called *Evangelical Herald.* One of the organizers of the Caroline Mission, he was 48 years old when the United States entered the war.

THE SYNOD AND THE EXTERNAL THREAT

The pastor working as camp visitor at Camp Lewis, Washington, reported a problem to the War Welfare Commission of the Evangelical Synod in January, 1918:

> Two of my men, both from our congregation, complained about receiving publications plainly showing that they are issued by a German organization. They most likely mean the '*Herald*' published by 'German Evang. Synod' etc. They have heard remarks at Camp Lewis about this mail which they receive, and they would hate to become marked men or be held in suspicion even in the slightest degree since they are anxious to advance.[99]

This was not the only report received by the Commission of discomfort felt by soldiers receiving literature with the word "German" on the masthead. William Dresel, Chairman of the Commission, wrote to the officers of the Synod pleading for a name change, that the Synod's soldiers not be "open to misinterpretation, misunderstanding, criticism and possibly suspicion." Dresel continued:

> Even tho the recent General Conference voted otherwise, it seems wise that the Officers of our church, who certainly have the welfare of the entire church at heart, should take the matter of simplifying the official title of our denomination under advisement, obtain the necessary legal advice and proceed with the change immediately, if possible....And it does not seem expedient to wait another four months....[100]

John Baltzer gathered an informal meeting of district presidents and Synod officers on February 7. He pointed out the problem of the denomination's name, both for publications received in the camps and also on the ordination certificates of pastors applying to be chaplains. He reminded them that the movement to change the name preceded the war, but that the name could only be legally changed by an amendment process that would take years. He said,

> I assume that there is nobody among us who is ashamed of the name of our church, and who for this reason would change its name. But there will be only a few among us who do not feel that in this time the word 'German' leaves a bad taste not only with responsible government circles, but that it carries also a 'red cloth' effect with our young people.... Thus for strictly pastoral reasons it would be preferable if the word 'German' could be dropped.[101]

The name of the denomination could not be legally changed on such short notice. The *Evangelical Herald* simply dropped the denominational name from its masthead. In unofficial usage, the word "German" was dropped.

At the same meeting on February 7, Baltzer also asked if the district meetings scheduled for the Spring should be cancelled. He explained,

> These conferences are meetings of German pastors and German lay people. German is almost exclusively the language of those meetings. In certain circles the German Evangelical Synod of North America is viewed as the church of the German Kaiser in this country.[102]

Baltzer went on to say these conferences would attract super-patriots looking for spies. He also noted that some pastors and lay people liked to pronounce their solutions to political problems but "loquacity and imprudence are closely related," and one arrest would do great harm to the standing of the Synod.

Only three districts held their conferences. Elsewhere Synod leaders met with smaller clusters of pastors to address necessary business.

Many states and communities expressed hostility to the use of the German language; a few took action. Montana banned the use of German in the pulpit. South Dakota prohibited the use of German on the telephone and in meetings of three or more persons.[103] The Iowa governor prohibited the use of any language other than English in schools, in conversation in public places, in public addresses and public worship.[104] According to one source, thirty Evangelical Synod pastors were forced to resign because they could not preach in English.[105]

One pastor wrote to President Baltzer proposing that the Synod print an English sermon each week, to be distributed to pastors, so that those who could not compose their thoughts in English could read the sermon.[106] Another pastor wrote to the Seminary Board with his ideas on how to make Elmhurst English speaking if required.[107] I am not aware of anything being done on the first suggestion. Elmhurst did proceed to become English speaking, but not immediately.

The accusation that the Evangelical Synod was the Kaiser's church came most frequently from Missouri Synod Lutherans. In Prussia the government had persecuted "Old Lutherans" who refused to enter the United Lutheran-Reformed State Church. Old Lutheran refugees organized the Missouri Synod. Missouri and Evangelical Synods competed for the loyalty of common waves of immigrants settling in the same places. To the Missouri Synod, the Evangelical Synod was an extension of the church that persecuted them. Because Missouri Synod pastors would not join in events where others led in prayer, they often did not participate in rallies in support of the war, and therefore came under suspicion of disloyalty. In their defense, they pointed the finger at the Evangelical Synod and called it the Kaiser's church.

The Evangelical Synod had to shift gears. Before the war they often spoke of the German Union Churches as their "mother church" and welcomed immigrants from those churches to the Synod. Now they had to emphasize their separateness—the Evangelical Synod was a distinct, democratic American church with no lines of accountability to Germany. This about-face came across as hypocritical, even to some members of the Synod.

When Reinhold Niebuhr learned that a pastor applying to be a chaplain was rejected because he was believed to belong to the State Church of Germany, Niebuhr asked Synod officials to prepare a pamphlet "setting forth the historical facts about our church."[108]

At Baltzer's request, seminary professor Samuel Press prepared the pamphlet. Then Press, Baltzer, and a couple of other leaders visited local gatherings of Synod pastors, distributed the pamphlets, and explained the Synod position.[109] Local pastors needed to be able to articulate the distinction and respond to attacks in a consistent manner.

Two weeks after Fontana's conviction, President Baltzer wrote to the members of the Synod's Supreme Judiciary with the question, "If a pastor is convicted and sent to prison, what form of procedure must the District observe?"[110] After a flurry of correspondence the Supreme Judiciary issued an opinion: "A clergyman or member of the synod found guilty of disloyalty by a Federal Court should suffer the same penalty at the hands of his district officers as would be inflicted upon him were he found guilty of murder, robbery, or some better known offence."[111] In the opinion of the Judiciary, a pastor convicted of disloyalty would be suspended while appeals proceeded through the courts. If the conviction was sustained by the higher courts, the pastor would be expelled.

In fact this did not happen. The Synod supported its pastors through every step of the legal process. Dr. Paul Krusius was described in the Pennsylvania District minutes as "now serving as camp chaplain for the interned."[112] The War Welfare Commission appropriated $1500 for his work as "voluntary chaplain" at Fort Oglethorpe.[113] Wilhelm Schumann continued to serve his Iowa congregation, and participated in the dedication of its new edifice, in spite of conviction for espionage and charges of assault.

John Fontana returned to his parish duties after church members posted bail. One of his first acts was to preside at the funeral of a soldier who died in France. At the request of his District President, he preached at the rededication of the Evangelical Church at Hebron, North Dakota, on August 25. Some church members at New Salem, surprised that Fontana resumed his duties while his case was being appealed, caused a congregational meeting to be held on September 1, to vote on his removal. The following is based on the report of BI Agent A. F. Kearney, sent to New Salem on September 18 to investigate:

> Fontana then spoke on his own behalf, and said that he was convicted because he had spoken, preached, prayed and sang in German and carried the impression that the object was to get the German out of the church.[114]

The congregation voted 57-22 to keep Fontana. Soon Fontana supporters were boycotting the businesses of Fontana opponents. However, Agent Kearney reported, "His sermons have been loyal and he has every time prayed for the success of the United States."[115]

Outside New Salem, newspapers reacted strongly against Fontana's endorsement from his congregation and his denomination, explicit in his invitation to preach at Hebron. The *New York Times,* basing its information on a report in the Grand Forks *Herald,* reported, "The seriousness of such a case as this lies... in its revelation that there exists a large ecclesiastical organization in the eyes of whose elected leaders' disloyalty constitutes a claim to honor...." The article concluded,

> It is the opinion of the Grand Forks paper that every member of that organization in North Dakota, at any rate, will stand a lot of watching by neighbors who have a right to call themselves Americans. That seems a reasonable suggestion and not at all harsh.[116]

The congregations supported their pastors, and the Synod, whatever its official legal position might be, could not abandon its faithful servants of the Gospel.

WAR & PEACE IN THE SYNOD

Eden student Thomas Marshall wrote in the student newspaper *Keryx* in December, 1917, "war is...nothing but legalized, organized murder."[117] This student was not opposing participation in the Great War, but saw it as a sign of dysfunction in international relations that needed to be ended. Nevertheless, his article reflected a deep and broad sentiment among clergy against war.

Reinhold Niebuhr addressed the students in the October 1918 issue of *Keryx*. He first recognized, "most ministers were or are pacifists."[118] Niebuhr criticized pacifism at that time as unpractical, explained that pacifists had to make compromises, and questioned the sincerity of those who opposed the Great War, but not all war: "The only possible cause for opposition to this war is a very genuine opposition to all war because as wars go there has never been one that had in it so much Christian idealism and that was so full of purpose to use the sacrifices of war for its final abolition."[119]

The peace movement had been growing in American Protestantism before the Great War. Most "pacifists" were not non-resisters, but were advocates of world order. They agreed with the American Peace Society goals of creating alternative non-violent means by which states could resolve conflict. When the United States entered "the war to end all wars," many of these pacifists supported the moral aims of the war because of President Wilson's idealism. However, Niebuhr was probably right for his denomination, "most ministers were or are pacifists."

In the late winter and early spring of 1917, as the United States broke diplomatic relations with Germany, and the English-language press beat the drums of war, Julius Horstmann editorialized in the Synod's *Evangelical Herald* against such action. He echoed the appeals of Socialists and other protestors that war would only profit big business, that there should be a national referendum on the war, and that "freedom of speech must be exercised."[120] He saw the country sliding into war because its so-called "neutrality" had actually been a non-objective support of England.[121] In Holy Week, the day before war was declared, he wrote,

> These are days of trouble and tribulation for all who desire peace and righteousness. The very word 'peace' is under a cloud and those who desire to have and to keep peace for the nation and for the world must be ready to endure ridicule and even persecution....May the spirit of the Prince of Peace rule in the minds, heart, hands and lips of all who realize that strife and war is never an honor for any people, and that no war has ever brought a real and lasting peace. The forces that make for war are the allied hosts of wickedness: national selfishness; malignant falsehood; cold, calculating mammonism; the lust to kill and to destroy; the cruel, reckless ambition for power and conquest, on land or sea, or for the control of trade.[122]

As the country moved into war, Horstmann reported on the activities of the anti-war "People's Council for Democracy and Peace."[123] At the time of the first draft registration, Horstmann defended the rights of conscientious objectors, including those whose objection was to this particular war.[124] He appealed to the church leaders and pastors to speak boldly:

> There is a great need of real prophetic leadership in this hour, of men who are not afraid to lift up their voice and make it heard throughout the nation in opposition to the spirit of the times.... Where is the prophet who, like Isaiah, dares to brave the madness of mammonism's devotees or the unthinking masses who permit the newspapers, the tools of 'Big Business' to guide their thinking and their conduct? [125]

As all denominations were being pressured to fall in line in support of the war, Horstmann wrote,

> The world has become accustomed to war by thousands of years of cruel and bloody conflict. So-called Christian nations have continually been at war with each other. War has been carried on in behalf of the Church, and the Church herself has sometimes engaged in war. But all this does not change in the least the fact that warfare is un-Christian and therefore incompatible with the principles and aims for which the Church must stand if she desires to remain true to her Founder, Head and Lord, and to herself. The Churches therefore have every right to be opposed to war on principle.... It follows from this that the Church as such cannot be expected to support war or war measures, or to encourage or promote anything that may be construed as an approval of war.[126]

At the end of the month in which the Pomeroy church was burned, he decried, "indiscriminate, un-American and un-Christian attacks...upon everything that bore the name German."[127] He took issue with a statement that, "the Church ought to show herself the faithful servant of the nation," insisting that, while it is the duty of individual Christians to obey the government, the Church is the servant of Jesus Christ alone.[128]

The *Evangelical Herald* devoted its April 18, 1918, issue to the War Welfare Commission, with which Commission Secretary Reinhold Niebuhr was at first "entirely satisfied."[129] However when Pastor Arne Franke was denied access to Camp Funston because of Horstmann's editorial in that issue, which criticized censorship, Niebuhr wrote to Horstmann, "I think all of those articles about the press and the truth served no good purpose in a German American paper and they may result in our publications being banned from the camps."[130] The War Welfare Commission on May 1 adopted the following resolutions:

RESOLUTION NO. 6

Resolved that we, the War Welfare Commission, disavow the editorial in the *Evangelical Herald* of April 18th, express to the editor our regret over the publication of an editorial which is not unequivocally loyal and that we urge upon him the adoption of an editorial policy of unqualified patriotism.

RESOLUTION NO. 7

In view of the fact that articles have appeared in the official organs of our Church warranting the accusation that our Synod has not been as loyal as it should be, be it resolved that we, the War Welfare Commission, hereby urge upon the Editorial Commission (Rev. J. Baltzer, chairman) to take stricter surveillance over the policy in our denominational publications and to take such steps as necessary to guarantee an unequivocal American attitude in our periodicals.

RESOLUTION NO. 8

Voted to ask our editors to sound a positive and unmistakable note of loyalty in the publications of our Church. Let this be dictated by a sense of duty and loyalty and not merely by necessity. Try to convince others that we are loyal by positively endorsing the principles of our government in this war.[131]

On May 10 Niebuhr reported to the Commission that Rev. Paul Crusius was refused a chaplaincy because the secret service believed the Evangelical Synod to be disloyal, based on editorials in the *Herald*. Niebuhr concluded, "All this proves that most drastic action is necessary."[132]

Horstmann's May 9 editorial, "What Is Loyalty?" discussed a speech by Robert E. Speer, Chairman of the General War-Time Commission of the Churches, in which he pointed out some of America's national shortcomings. Horstmann also discussed the reaction to his speech characterized by angry accusations of disloyalty, and Speer's response. Horstmann concluded, "only a people conscious and penitent for their own sins have any right to go out and administer chastisement to others."[133] Niebuhr reacted in a crisp letter to Horstmann, "You have, as far as I know, never breathed one word of criticism against the German government, while you have often criticized our own."[134]

The tension appears to have cooled off for a while. Horstmann used his editorial column to emphasize that the Evangelical Synod was not the Kaiser's church,[135] and to explain that the use of German in the Evangelical Synod was a temporary condition, but force should not be used to require English.[136]

On September 27, 1918, Reinhold Niebuhr again wrote to Horstmann, complaining that Horstmann had taken parts of an article Niebuhr had sent, and twisted its sense, and didn't give credit. Niebuhr again expressed his discomfort with Horstmann's editorial policy.[137] Horstmann apologized,[138] and Niebuhr apologized for jumping to conclusions, but repeated his concern over "subtle anti-American insinuations" in his editorials. Niebuhr continued:

> But your attitude toward every American war measure is entirely critical and never sympathetic. Nor have you ever spoken one word in your column that would lead any reader to believe that you favored the American war aims, even any portion or part of them.[139]

Horstmann replied, "...whatever matters I do discuss editorially I aim to consider entirely from an unbiased Christian point of view...let the chips fall where they may." He continued,

> I do not see, however, that there need be any conflict between real Americanism and a Christian conscience. Tho there is a great gulf fixed between the spirit of Jesus Christ and many evil

forces and tendencies parading under the guise of American-ism. Ever since we are at war I have been very careful not to criticize the Government or its war measures; I have, however, felt it my duty to be very outspoken in my condemnation of the know-nothing mob spirit and the hysteria of super-patri-otism which infested the newspapers and infected too large a proportion of our people.[140]

Meanwhile, David Brunning, Vice President of the Synod, wrote to Synod President John Baltzer on October 12, complaining about both the *Friedensbote* and the *Herald*.

Together with me, a number of brethren have missed in our weeklies a clear statement of the support of our Evangelical Church of the President in the issues of war as he has laid them down. There has always been a string to every 'patriotic' utter-ance of both of them. I am totally disgusted again. I am going to try my level best to get both of them out of their jobs since I doubt their loyalty to our country.[141]

Within a month the war ended; no one got fired.

Niebuhr and Horstmann had a great deal in common: both second-generation Americans, reared in the Evangelical Synod, eager to bring it into the American mainstream, and both espousing liberal political views. Niebuhr, age 25, eager to make his denomination 100% American, and inspired by the idealism of President Wilson, set aside his pacifist leanings to support the war. Horstmann, age 48, had a keener awareness of the dark side of patriotism and the demonic nature of war.

AFTER THE WAR

The Great War was the threshold of the twentieth century. Empires fell; new nations arose; millions had died; no one seemed to know why. The world would never be the same. The crisis experienced by German Americans in general, and the Evangelical Synod in particular, would also shape the future of individuals and institutions.

Pastor **John Reichardt** did not return to Lowden, Iowa, after the riot. District Attorney O'Connor wrote to the Attorney General's office on March 12, 1919, proposing that charges be dropped, as the war was over. On October 8, 1919, the government filed a motion for dismissal.[142] According to the clergy card file at Eden Archives, John Reichardt served a church at Morrison, Missouri, from 1919 to 1928. However, I do not find him there in the 1920 Census; I find no further record of him.

Dr. **Paul Krusius**, after his stay at Fort Oglethorpe, was deported to Germany in 1919. He found his homeland immersed in poverty, hunger and despair. The Evangelical Synod of North America responded generously with funds and material aid for the poor and suffering of Germany, and Dr. Krusius coordinated this relief work for the six years it lasted.[143] Krusius was soon holding down three jobs. In addition to the relief work, he began on August 1, 1919, to teach at a school in the Francke Foundation at Halle, and taught at their schools until February 1, 1925. He also directed the German Home at Halle, established in 1920 as a boarding school for orphans and expatriate Germans.[144] He continued to direct the Home until August 5, 1932. Students experienced "a home in the truest sense of the word."[145] Following this work he apparently went into pastoral work.

The case of Pastor **John Fontana**, of New Salem, North Dakota, was appealed. The Eighth Circuit Court of Appeals reversed the judgment on December 8, 1919, and directed the lower court to discharge the defendant. In the circuit court's opinion (1) the indictment was not precise enough in its charges to give the defense the opportunity to prepare adequately, and (2) there was insufficient evidence to prove he committed a crime.[146] John Fontana continued to serve Peace Evangelical Church, New Salem, until 1925. He then served other congregations, finally St. John's Evangelical congregation of Rogers Corners, near Chelsea, Michigan, for fourteen years until his retirement and death in 1953.[147]

Pastor **Wilhelm Schumann's** case was appealed, but was rejected by the Court of Appeals on April 28, 1919, and the Supreme Court on October 13, 1919.[148] Schumann surrendered to authorities at Fort Dodge, Iowa, on Monday, November 17, 1919, and began his five-year sentence at Leavenworth, Kansas, by the end of the week.[149] At Leavenworth, Schumann worked first in the clothing department, then in the dark room of the photography gallery. He declined to file an application for parole, although many Evangelical pastors and others signed a petition for executive clemency.[150]

After two years in prison, Pastor Schumann received a pardon from President Harding on Christmas 1921.[151] Schumann went first to his brother in Chicago. Pastor R. Lorenz, who had been serving the church at Pomeroy in Schumann's absence, brought the question of Schumann's return to the congregation at their annual meeting on January 2, 1922. The minutes state:

> Our pastor [Lorenz] referred now to Pastor William Schumann, who was given his freedom again, and requested our congregation to give the matter of calling him again to be their pastor kind consideration. He suggested that they notify every member by letter and then in all love (with the welfare of their congregation at heart) discuss this matter.[152]

Schumann evidently was not made to do time for his assault conviction in Iowa. He resumed his ministry at Pomeroy in 1922, and continued there until 1931. When I visited Pomeroy in 2006 I met two members who received Confirmation instruction from him and had fond memories of Pastor Schumann as one who was strict but fair. After Pomeroy, Pastor Schumann served Saint John's Evangelical Church of Montrose, Colorado, where he married, for the first time, in 1938, at the age of fifty-eight. He then served a Lutheran Church at New Castle, Colorado, where he lived for sixteen years, and died in 1954.[153]

The people at Pomeroy associated with the United Church of Christ (formerly the Evangelical Church) told me that the three alleged arsonists responsible for burning down the church all died terrible deaths—suicides and accidents—within two years of the fire.[154] These events appear to reassure the faithful that there is divine justice after all.

Herman Hahn served Salem Evangelical Church, Buffalo, New York, for twenty-six years and molded it into a "working man's church." Always a controversial figure, and a frequent Socialist candidate for political office, he died in 1948.

Judge **Charles F. Amidon**, who had protected free speech in many other cases, but scolded John Fontana for not having an "American soul," was exhausted by the stresses of the Espionage Act cases. His daughter reflected, "some mainspring of vigor had snapped."[155] He continued as a judge for ten more years, and lived ten more years after retirement, widely hailed as a defender of free speech.

The Evangelical Synod healed and forged ahead after the war, in its process of Americanization, and along some new twists in the road.

Language. The church in Lowden, Iowa, began using some English in worship in 1919. At New Salem, North Dakota, Peace Church began using English in worship in 1920, although minutes were kept in German until 1933. The church at Pomeroy, Iowa, began English worship in 1928. In the period from 1913 to 1920 the proportion of Evangelical Synod churches using only English in Sunday School rose from 25% to 59%.[156] By 1920, 42% of Synod worship services were in English.[157] General Conference minutes by 1927 were all in English.

Accreditation. Helmut R. Niebuhr, brother of Reinhold, led the campaign to upgrade the Evangelical Synod's educational institutions. Helmut Niebuhr served as President of Elmhurst College from 1924 to 1927, and Academic Dean of Eden Seminary from 1927 to 1930. Elmhurst upgraded to a Junior College in 1920, had a four-year program by 1925, and received accreditation in 1934. Eden also expanded its program and upgraded its standards.[158]

Denominational name. The General Conference of 1921 debated for two days a proposal to take the word "German" out of the name of the denomination. The resolution passed, but opponents appealed to the Synod's Supreme Judiciary, which ruled the action unconstitutional.[159] Not until 1927 was the word finally removed, by a slower constitutional process.[160]

Relations with the church in Germany. The Evangelical Synod shared with the Evangelical Union churches of Germany a unionist doctrinal foundation, and many immigrants from those churches that joined the Synod. However, the Synod's early pastors were sent out by continental missionary societies that shared the Lutheran-Reformed unionist vision of the Evangelical churches of Germany, but were not organizationally connected to them. The Evangelical Synod affirmed its association with the "mother church" in Germany before the war, and did its best to distance itself from the "Kaiser's church" during the war. After the war, the Synod engaged in major relief work in Germany. For the first time, the Evangelical Synod was relating directly to the continent through the churches (*landeskirchen*) rather than through the missionary societies. Trips of church leaders from both continents, to visit their fellow religionists across the Atlantic, helped to build a sense of identity. The American churches offered to the German churches much-needed relief in a time of distress. The American Synod looked to the relationship as an opening to theological renewal from the more academic and intellectual German church. After the war, the Evangelical Synod developed closer ties with the German churches than it ever had before.

Peace. The Evangelical Synod experienced, along with the rest of Western Civilization, a post-war disillusionment with war. The "war to end all wars" didn't. Nothing to come out of the war seemed to justify its enormous cost in human suffering. Reinhold Niebuhr was one of many who renounced war and returned to pacifism.[161] The Evangelical Synod, which never had as bad a case of war fever as the Anglo denominations, soon expressed strong peace sentiments. The 1924 *Synod Reports* contained a statement on the church and war. The statement looked back with horror on the war just passed, and contemplated how the church might better respond in a future war. It recognized both the Christian's responsibility to obey the state (*Romans 13:1*), and the calling to obey God rather than men (*Acts 5:29*). It declared:

> According to the sentiment of the people and the teachings of the Church, war is in direct opposition to the Church....The Church regards war as a monstrous evil, as the triumphal march or as the power of the arch enemy of the Church which destroys its peace.[162]

The report concluded, "no pastor belongs upon an Evangelical pulpit who uses his pulpit for preaching or inciting hatred or enmity against other nations."[163]

General Conference in 1925, in a resolution on the Outlawry of War, echoed the ideas of the Kellogg-Briand pact, and also declared, "We will not, as a Christian Church, ever bless or sanction war."[164]

Ecumenism. The war gave a boost to greater cooperation and union among churches. Many looked at the disunity of the church as one reason its voice could not be heard in opposition to entry into war. For the Evangelical Synod, union with older denominations would also facilitate the process of Americanization, and the vision of Christian unity had always shaped the Synod's identity. Helmut Niebuhr chaired the Synod's Commission on Closer Relations with Other Church Bodies. Giving up on the prospect of union with Lutherans because of their confessionalism, the Synod turned to the Reformed Church of the United States, and in 1934 united with them to form the Evangelical and Reformed Church. This group united with the Congregational Christian Churches in 1957 to create the United Church of Christ.

Social Gospel. Julius Horstmann led in establishing a Commission on Christianity and Social Problems in the Missouri District. In 1925 the Synod established a Commission patterned after the one in Missouri. Reinhold Niebuhr served on this commission, chaired by Horstmann. They worked together on many issues of social concern in the life of the Synod.

Julius Horstmann continued editing denominational papers to 1941, giving articulate support to the Social Gospel, peace and Christian unity. He died in 1954. **Reinhold Niebuhr** became professor of ethics at Union Theological Seminary in New York in 1928, and retired from there in 1960. He became the leading American Protestant theologian of the middle third of the twentieth century. His theology of Christian realism revealed the marks of the Great War in his new consciousness of the power of sin, his distrust of idealism, and his willingness to get involved in the issues of the day in spite of their ethical ambiguities. He died in 1971. Reinhold's brother, Helmut, taught at Yale Divinity School from 1931 to 1962, where he used his less Germanic middle name, **H. Richard Niebuhr.** His concern over the limitations of his denomination's ethnic identity found expression in his *Social Sources of Denominationalism* (1929), in which he advocated a Christian unity that transcended ethnicity, class, race and region.

The trauma of the Great War soon ended. Pastors and churches returned to normalcy as best they could. But life would never be the same. The younger generation of the Synod carried forward the giant boost the war had given to Americanization, as their elders reluctantly gave way. A concern for peace that did not entirely die out in the war, recovered with vigor, and would endure. The Synod would never be as isolated again, reaching out to form church unions in this country, establishing closer ties—on an equal footing—with the German churches, and through the Niebuhr brothers claiming a place in the mainstream of American Protestant theology.

Closing Reflection

A massive propaganda campaign to convince the country to go to war; vilification of the enemy leading to acts of violence against an immigrant community; trials of questionable integrity against members of that immigrant community: Is this a description of 1917 or 2002? The answer is both. We have not learned from history and so we repeat it. Certainly members of the religious and ethnic communities that were bullied in the streets and courtrooms a hundred years ago, should be sensitive to the similar experience of others today.

ENDNOTES

1. National Archives and Records Administration (NARA), Kansas City Center. Record Group (RG) 21: Records of the United States District Court for the Northern District of Iowa, Criminal Case Files (1890-1962), file 1260, Reichardt, John (*U.S. v. Reichardt*).

2. NARA, College Park, MD, Center. General Records of the Department of Justice, Classified Subjects File, 9-16-12-788 (*Krusius*).

3. NARA, Kansas City Center. RG 21: Records of the United States District Court for the District of North Dakota, All Divisions, Fargo, North Dakota, Criminal Cases (1890-1957). Case 2831, United States v. J. Fontana (*U.S. v. Fontana*).

4. NARA, Kansas City Center, RG 21: Records of the United States District Court for the Northern District of Iowa, Central Division, Fort Dodge, IA, Criminal cases (1882-1968). Case 1202, and Eastern Division, Dubuque, IA, Criminal Cases (1863-1962) File 4286 (*U.S. v. Schumann*).

5. See Stephen Vaughn, *Holding Fast the Inner Lines: Democracy, Nationalism, and the Committee on Public Information* (Chapel Hill, NC: University of North Carolina Press, 1980).

6. See Joan M. Jensen, *The Price of Vigilance* (Chicago: Rand McNally & Co., 1968).

7. Quoted in Zechariah Chafee, Jr., *Free Speech in the United States* (Cambridge, MA: Harvard University Press, 1948), 39.

8. Hugo Kamphausen, *The Story of the Religious Life in the Evangelical Synod of North America* (St. Louis: Eden Publishing House, 1924), 163-64.

9. NARA, M1085. Investigative Reports of the Bureau of Investigation 1908-1922: Old German Files 1909-1921. Case 8000-16213: Rev. John Reichardt. Report, 14 May 1917. Accessed through www.fold3.com on 11 July 2012.

10. Ibid.

11. NARA, Reichardt Investigation. Report, William W. Rost, 29 May 1917.

12. NARA, M1085. Investigative Reports of the Bureau of Investigation 1908-1922: Old German Files 1909-1921. Case 8000-9884: Rev. John Fontana. Report, H. G. Garber, 19 April 1917. Accessed through www.fold3.com on 11 July 2012.

13. Ibid.

14. *Krusius.* Summary Sheet for Disposal of Interned Alien Enemy.

15. NARA, M1085. Investigative Reports of the Bureau of Investigation 1908-1922: Old German Files 1909-1921. Case 8000-78958: Rev. Wilhelm Schumann. Report, A. P. Sherwood, 26 October 1917. Accessed through www.fold3.com on 11 July 2012.

16. NARA, Schumann Investigation. Report, M. Eberstein, 25 November 1917.

17. NARA, M1085. Investigative Reports of the Bureau of Investigation 1908-1922: Old German Files 1909-1921. Case 8000-108036: R. Niebuhr. Report, B. C. Baldwin, 9 December 1917. Accessed through www.fold3.com on 11 July 2012.

18. Ibid.

19. Crawford, Kenneth G., "Rev. Herman J. Hahn." In *He Stirreth Up the People: The Social Implications of the Teachings of Jesus,* by Herman J. Hahn (Buffalo: Salem Evangelical Brotherhood, 1931), p. 5. Eden Theological Seminary, Saint Louis, MO, Eden Archives (EA). Congregation files: New York, Buffalo, Salem Evangelical.

20. NARA, M1085. Investigative Reports of the Bureau of Investigation 1908-1922: Old German Files 1909-1921. Case 8000-181057: Rev. Hahn. Report, L. M. Cantrell, 20 April 1918. Accessed through www.fold3.com on 11 July 2012.

21. Crawford, p. 5.

22. NARA, Hahn investigation. Report, M. P. Cantillon, 8 May 1918.

23. *U.S. v. Reichardt,* Indictment.

24. Nancy Derr, "Lowden: A Study of Intolerance in an Iowa Community During the Era of the First World War," *The Annals of Iowa* 50:1 (Summer 1989): 8.

25. *U.S. v. Fontana,* Indictment.

26. *U.S. v. Schumann,* Indictment.

27. *Fort Dodge Messenger and Chronicle,* Dec 4, 1917, p. 1.

28. Ibid., Dec 24, 1917, p. 2; quoted from *Pomeroy Herald.*

29. Ibid.

30. First Evangelical Church of Pomeroy, *Minutes.*

31. *Fort Dodge Messenger,* Jan 9, 1918, p. 1.

32. Letter. Henry Moulton to Herma Wiggins, June 19, 2003. Fort Dodge Historical Society. Also conversations of the author with parishioners.

33. Letter. Ralph Wedeking to Eden Archives, 24 July 2003. Evangelical Synod of North America, Archives. Eden Theological Seminary, Saint Louis, MO (EA). Congregation files: Iowa, Pomeroy, First; also Green County, Iowa. Clerk of Courts. Box 241, file # 67. State of Iowa v. Wilhelm Schumanm (*Iowa v. Schumann*).

34. *Iowa v. Schumann.*

35. Derr, "Lowden," 13-14.

36. Georgiana Pell Curtis and Benedict Elder, eds., *The American Catholic Who's Who,* vol. 7 (1946-1947): 340; Randolph W. Lyon, *Encyclopedia Dubuque,* "O'Connor, Frank Aloysius." http://www.encyclopediadubuque. org, Accessed 19 February 2011; James Clark Fifield, ed., *The American Bar: Contemporary Lawyers of the United States and Canada* (Minneapolis: James C. Fifield Co., 1918), 197. O'Connor later became active in the Roosevelt administration as counsel, and then general agent, for the Farm Credit Administration, and at the Democratic Convention in 1940 placed in nomination for vice president the name of Henry Wallace.

37. North Dakota State University: Institute for Regional Studies, "Melvin A. Hildreth" http://www.lib.ndsu.nodak.edu/ndirs/collections/manuscripts/legal/Hildreth/index.html, Accessed 20 July 2006; Michael Robert Patterson, webmaster, Arlington National Cemetery Website. "Melvin A. Hildreth" http://www.arlingtoncemetery.net /mahildreth.htm. Accessed 18 February 2011.

38. I. Kenneth Smemo, "Progressive Judge: The Public Career of Charles Fremont Amidon," (Ph.D. diss., University of Minnesota, 1967), 257.

39. Ibid., 200.

40. Edgar Rubey Harlan, *A Narrative History of the People of Iowa*, vol. 4 (Chicago: American Historical Society, 1931), transcribed at http://archiver.rootsweb.ancestry.com/th/read/IOWA/2010-02/1265362529. Accessed 19 February 2011; Iowa Legislature http://www.legis/gov/Legislators/legislatorAllYears.aspx?PID=3318. Accessed 18 February 2011.

41. North Dakota Supreme Court Justices, "John Knauf." http:www.court.state.nd.us/court/bios/knauf.htm. Accessed 20 July 2006; William S. Hein, *Bench and Bar*, 116, Heinonline. http://heinonline.org/HOL/LandingPage?collection=journals&handle=hein.journals/nordak29&div=20&id=&page=. Accessed 19 February 2011; Curt Eriksmoen, "Attorney stood up to challenges" *Bismarck Tribune*, Nov. 1, 2009. http://www.bismarcktribune.com/news/columnists/article_c6c41e46-c696-11de-a13e-001cc4c002e0.html. Accessed 20 February 2011.

42. Eriksmoen.

43. Biographical Dictionary of Federal Judges, "Reed, Henry Thomas," http://www.fjc.gov/servlet/tGetInfo?jid=1979. Accessed 20 July 2006.

44. Chafee, *Freedom of Speech in the United States* (1948), 50.

45. Geoffrey R. Stone, *Perilous Times: Free Speech in Wartime: From the Sedition Act of 1798 to the War on Terrorism* (New York: W. W. Norton & Co., 2004), 160.

46. Walter Nelles, ed., *Espionage Court Cases, With Certain Others on Related Points* (New York: National Civil Liberties Bureau, July 1918), 90-91.

47. Jeffrey Brandon Morris, *Establishing Justice in Middle America: A History of the United States Court of Appeals for the Eighth Circuit* (Minneapolis: University of Minnesota Press, 2007), 92.

48. Quoted in Smemo, 278.

49. Beulah Amidon Ratliff, "Charles Fremont Amidon, 1856-1937," *North Dakota History* 8 (Jan 1941): 99.

50. *U.S. v. Schumann,* 66-68; Evangelical Synod Archives. Pastor files: Schuman(n), Wilhelm.

51. *U.S. v. Fontana,* 290-91; Evangelical Synod Archives. Pastor files: Fontana, John.

52. It was the 434th anniversary of Luther's birth, in the 400th year of the Reformation.

53. *U.S. v. Schumann,* 71.

54. Ibid.

55. Ibid., 45.

56. Ibid., 57-58.

57. Ibid., 80-81.

58. Ibid., 84.

59. Ibid., 85-86.

60. Ibid., 87-88.

61. Ibid., 110.

62. Ibid., 84-86.

63. Ibid., 159.

64. *U.S. v. Fontana,* demurrer.

65. John D. Lawson, ed. "The Trial of John Fontana for Disloyalty, Bismarck, North Dakota, 1918," *American State Trials,* 12:897-961 (Saint Louis: F. H. Thomas Law Book Co., 1914-1936, reprint, Wilmington, DE: Scholarly Resources, Inc., 1972), 902.

66. *U.S. v. Fontana,* 6-9.

67. Ibid., 188-90.

68. Ibid., 5; italics mine.

69. Ibid., 200.

70. Ibid., 49, 236-37.

71. Ibid., 28, 209.

72. Ibid., 162-64.

73. Ibid., 18.

74. Ibid., 202.

75. Ibid., 228.

76. Lawson, 938-39.

77. Ibid., 943.

78. *U.S. v. Fontana,* 254.

79. *Bismarck Tribune,* 2 August 1918, 1.

80. *U.S. v. Fontana,* 289.

81. For example, *New York Times,* 15 September 1918, 4:8.

82. *U.S. v. Fontana,* 292-97.

83. John P. Roche, *The Quest for the Dream: The Development of Civil Rights and Human Relations in Modern America* (New York: Macmillan, 1963), 43.

84. Other accounts of anti-German feeling include: Leola Allen, "Anti-German Sentiment in Iowa During World War I," *Annals of Iowa* 42:6 (1974): 418-29; Tina Stewart Brakebill, "From 'German Days' to '100 Percent Americanism,'" *Journal of the Illinois State Historical Society* 95:2 (2002): 148-71; Lyle W. Dorsett, "The Ordeal of Colorado's Germans During World War 1," *The Colorado Magazine* 51:4 (1874): 277-293; Matthew Goode, "'Obey the Law and Keep Your Mouths Shut': German Americans in Grand Rapids During World War I," *Michigan History Magazine* 78 (Mar/Apr 1994): 19-23; Melvin G. Holli, "Teuton vs. Slav: The Great War Sinks Chicago's German *Kultur,*" *Ethnicity* 8:4 (1981): 406-51; Carl E. Krog, "The Battle Against the Kaiser: Social and Cultural Conflict in Marinette, Wisconsin, During the World War I Era," *Yearbook of German-American Studies* 26 (1991): 231-47; Thomas Reimer, "Distant Thunder: The

German-American Clergy of Schenectady, New York, and the European War, 1914-1917," *New York History* 73:3 (Jul 1992): 291-320; Chris Richardson, "With Liberty and Justice for All?: The Suppression of German-American Culture During World War I," *Missouri Historical Review* 90:1 (1995): 79-89; Clifford H. Scott, "Assimilation in a German-American Community: The Impact of World War I," *Northwest Ohio Quarterly* 52:1 (1980): 153-67; Mark Sonntag, "Fighting Everything German in Texas, 1917-1919," *Historian* 56:4 (Summer 1994): 656-70; Theodore F. Straub, "Eureka During World War I," *Der Stammbaum: Germans from Russia Heritage Society Heritage Review* 11:1 (Feb 1981): 2-4 (This is a chapter from *Autobiography of Theodore F. Straub*); Steven Wrede, "The Americanization of Scott County, 1914-1918," *The Annals of Iowa* 44:8 (1979): 627-38.

85. Roche, 44.

86. Information on Krusius is from the archives of the Franke Foundation, as reported in electronic mail from J. Gröschl, Franke Foundation archivist, to William D. Meyer, and also in J. Lowry Maxwell, *Half a Century of Grace: A Jubilee History of the Sudan United Mission* (London, Sudan United Mission [1954]), 23-24, 101-03.

87. Electronic mail, Scott Holl, Eden Seminary archivist, to William Meyer, February 13, 2020. See also *Keryx* 7:1 (February 1917): 20.

88. NARA, Krusius. Letter. P. Krusius to T. W. Gregory. 5 November 1917.

89. NARA, Krusius. Letter. P. Krusius to Attorney General. 22 May 1919.

90. Ibid.

91. Kamphausen, 192, gives 1921 figures: 1,023 congregations with 274,800 members.

92. William C. Chrystal, "Reinhold Niebuhr and the First World War," *Journal of Presbyterian History* 55:3 (1977): 288-89.

93. Margaret Renton, ed., *War-Time Agencies of the Churches: Directory and Handbook* (New York: General War-Time Commission of the Churches, Federal Council of Churches of Christ in America, 1919), 44-45.

94. Julius H. Horstmann, "The Rise of the Social View-Point in the Evangelical Synod of North America," *Theological Magazine of the Evangelical Synod of North America* 62 (Sep 1934): 323.

95. Ibid., 324.

96. Ibid.

97. Ibid., 326; *Keryx* 7:1 (Feb 1917):17-19.

98. Horstmann, "Social View," 325; Kamphausen, 151-54.

99. EA, War Welfare Commission (WWC). Baltzer, J. to William Dresel. Letter. 9 January 1918.

100. EA, WWC. Dresel, William, to Officers of the Synod. Letter. 18 January 1918.

101. EA, Baltzer, John. Address, 7 February 1918. Translated by Stan Ehrlich.

102. Ibid.

103. Frederick C. Luebke, *Bonds of Loyalty: German Americans and World War I* (DeKalb, IL: Northern Illinois University, 1974), 252.

104. Nancy Ruth Derr, "Iowans During World War I: A Study of Change Under Stress," (Ph.D. diss, George Washington University, 1979), 494.

105. Luebke, 290.

106. EA, Baltzer correspondence. H. Manrodt to John Baltzer. Letter. 5 April 1918.

107. EA, Brunning correspondence. David Brunning to Seminary Board. Letter. 29 June 1918.

108. EA, WWC, Report of the Secretary, 10 May 1918.

109. EA, Baltzer correspondence. Baltzer, John, to A. H. Becker. Letter. 15 May 1918.

110. EA, Baltzer correspondence. Baltzer, John, to F. Hoffman. Letter. 20 August 1918.

111. EA, Baltzer correspondence. "Opinion of the Rights of Pastors Convicted of Disloyalty."

112. Evangelical Synod of North America (Ev. Syn.). *District Minutes* 1918: Pennsylvania, 5.

113. Ev. Syn. *Reports of the Synod Officers and Boards* 1918, 98.

114. NARA, Fontana investigation. Report, A. F. Kearney, 18 September 1918.

115. Ibid.

116. *New York Times,* 17 September 1918, 12.

117. *Keryx,* 7:5 (Dec 1917), 5.

118. *Keryx* 8:4 (Oct 1918), 2.

119. Ibid., 3.

120. *Evangelical Herald,* 16:7 (15 Feb 1917),1; 16:13 (29 Mar 1917), 1; 16:25 (21 Jun 1917), 1.

121. Ibid., 16:10 (8 Mar 1917), 1.

122. Ibid., 16:14 (5 Apr 1917), 1.

123. Ibid., 16:29 (19 Jul 1917), 1.

124. Ibid., 16:22 (31 May 1917), 1; 16:29 (19 July 1917), 1; 16:30 (26 Jul 1917),1.

125. Ibid., 16:25 (21 June 1917), 1; also 16:23 (7 June 1917), 1.

126. Ibid., 16:32 (9 Aug 1917), 1.

127. Ibid., 17:5 (31 Jan 1918), 1.

128. Ibid., 17:14 (4 Apr 1918), 1.

129. EA, WWC Correspondence, Reinhold Niebuhr to Julius Horstmann, 23 April 1918.

130. EA, Correspondence of Reinhold Niebuhr and Julius Horstmann, Niebuhr to Horstmann, 27 April 1918.

131. EA, WWC.

132. EA, WWC, Report of the Secretary, 10 May 1918.

133. *Evangelical Herald* 17:19 (9 May 1918), 1.

134. EA, Correspondence of Reinhold Niebuhr and Julius Horstmann, Niebuhr to Horstmann, 11 May 1918.

135. *Evangelical Herald* 17:27 (4 July 1918), 1.

136. Ibid., 17:30 (25 July 1918), 1.

137. EA, Correspondence of Reinhold Niebuhr and Julius Horstmann, Niebuhr to Horstmann, 27 Sep 1918.

138. Ibid., Horstmann to Niebuhr, 2 Oct 1918.

139. Ibid., Niebuhr to Horstmann, 4 Oct 1918.

140. Ibid., Horstmann to Niebuhr, 18 Oct 1918.

141. EA, Baltzer correspondence, Brunning to Baltzer, 12 Oct 1918.

142. *Reichardt v. U.S.*

143. Ev. Syn., General Conference Minutes, 1925: 49-50.

144. The home served 30 to 40 schoolchildren at a time. It had a family-like atmosphere and included workshops for manual skills and a garden for farming. "The German Home in the Francke Foundation," *Francke-Blätter,* 1997, no. 1. Translated by Mason Barnett.

145. Ibid.

146. *Fontana v. U.S.,* Eighth Circuit Court of Appeals, # 5295. LexisNexis Print Delivery, August 22, 2005.

147. EA, clergy files: Fontana, John.

148. *Schumann v. U.S.,* Eighth Circuit Court of Appeals, # 5275. Lexis-Nexis Print Delivery, August 22, 2005; and *Schumann v. U.S.,* Supreme Court of the United States, # 430. LexisNexis Print Delivery, August 22, 2005.

149. *Fort Dodge Messenger and Chronicle,* Nov. 18, 1919, 7; *U.S. v. Schumann.*

150. *U.S. v. Schumann,* including letter, Alfred E. Meyer to Parole Board, 7 July 1921.

151. *Fort Dodge Messenger and Chronicle,* 24 Dec 1921, 1.

152. First Evangelical Church of Pomeroy, *Minutes,* 243.

153. EA, clergy files, Schuman(n), Wilhelm.

154. Wedeking, Ralph, to Charles A. Maxfield. Electronic mail. 12 Apr 2004; and personal interviews.

155. Ratliff, 99.

156. Kamphausen, 166.

157. Ibid., 176.

158. Jon Diefenthaler, "H. Richard Niebuhr: A Fresh Look at His Early Years," *Church History* 52:2 (Je 1983): 176-77; Paul N. Crusius, "The Postwar Era," In *A History of the Evangelical and Reformed Church,* David Dunn, ed., 252-75 (Philadelphia: Christian Education, 1961), 252-59.

159. Kamphausen, 167.

160. Crusius, 275.

161. Richard Wightman Fox, *Reinhold Niebuhr: A Biography* (New York: Pantheon Books, 1985), 78.

162. Ev. Syn. *Reports,* 1924, 32.

163. Ibid., 33.

164. Ev. Syn., *General Conference Minutes,* 1925, 294.